Clara Ann Thompson

J. Pauline Smith

Mazie Earhart Clark

Voices in the Poetic Tradition

AFRICAN-AMERICAN WOMEN WRITERS, 1910–1940

HENRY LOUIS GATES, JR. *GENERAL EDITOR*

Jennifer Burton *Associate Editor*

OTHER TITLES IN THIS SERIES

CLARA ANN THOMPSON

J. PAULINE SMITH

MAZIE EARHART CLARK

VOICES IN THE POETIC TRADITION

Introduction by
MARY ANNE STEWART BOELCSKEVY

G. K. HALL & CO.
An Imprint of Simon & Schuster Macmillan
New York

Prentice Hall International
London   Mexico City   New Delhi   Singapore   Sydney   Toronto

G. K. Hall & Co.
An Imprint of Simon & Schuster Macmillan
1633 Broadway
New York, New York 10019

Library of Congress Catalog Card Number: [96-43472]

Printed in the United States of America

Printing Number
1   2   3   4   5   6   7   8   9   10

Library of Congress Cataloging-in-Publication Data

Thompson, Clara Ann.
    Voices in the poetic tradition / Clara Ann Thompson, J. Pauline Smith, Mazie Earhart Clark.
        p. cm. — (African-American women writers, 1910–1940)
        ISBN 0-7838-1430-5 (alk. paper)
        1. American poetry—Afro-American authors.   2. American poetry—Women authors.   3. Afro-American women—Poetry.   4. Afro-Americans—Poetry.
I. Smith, J. Pauline.   II. Clark, Mazie Earhart.
III. Title.   IV. Series.
PS3539.H645A6   1996
811'.520809287'08996073—dc20   96-43472
                                                    CIP

C O N T E N T S

GENERAL EDITORS' PREFACE

The past decade of our literary history might be thought of as the era of African-American women writers. Culminating in the awarding of the Pulitzer Prize to Toni Morrison and Rita Dove and the Nobel Prize for Literature to Toni Morrison in 1993 and characterized by the presence of several writers—Toni Morrison, Alice Walker, Maya Angelou, and the Delaney Sisters, among others—on the *New York Times* Best Seller List, the shape of the most recent period in our literary history has been determined in large part by the writings of black women.

This, of course, has not always been the case. African-American women authors have been publishing their thoughts and feelings at least since 1773, when Phillis Wheatley published her book of poems in London, thereby bringing poetry directly to bear upon the philosophical discourse over the African's "place in nature" and his or her place in the great chain of being. The scores of words published by black women in America in the nineteenth century—most of which were published in extremely limited editions and never reprinted—have been republished in new critical editions in the forty-volume *Schomburg Library of Nineteenth-Century Black Women Writers*. The critical response to that series has led to requests from scholars and students alike for a similar series, one geared to the work by black women·published between 1910 and the beginning of World War II.

African-American Women Writers, 1910–1940 is designed to bring back into print many writers who otherwise would be unknown to contemporary readers, and to increase the availability of lesser-known texts by established writers who originally published during this critical period in African-American letters. This series implicitly acts as a chronological sequel to the Schomburg series, which focused on the origins of the black female literary tradition in America.

In less than a decade, the study of African-American women's writings has grown from its promising beginnings into a firmly established field in departments of English, American Studies, and African-American Studies. A comparison of the form and function of the original series and this sequel illustrates this dramatic shift. The *Schomburg Library* was published at the cusp of focused academic investigation into the interplay between race and gender. It covered the extensive period from the publication of Phillis Wheatley's *Poems on Various Subjects, Religious and Moral* in 1773 through the "Black Women's Era" of 1890–1910, and was designed to be an inclusive series of the major early texts by black women writers. The Schomburg Library provided a historical backdrop for black women's writings of the 1970s and 1980s, including the works of writers such as Toni Morrison, Alice Walker, Maya Angelou, and Rita Dove.

African-American Women Writers, 1910–1940 continues our effort to provide a new generation of readers access to texts—historical, sociological, and literary—that have been largely "unread" for most of this century. The series bypasses works that are important both to the period and the tradition, but that are readily available, such as Zora Neale Hurston's *Their Eyes Were Watching God*, Jessie Fauset's *Plum Bun* and *There Is Confusion*, and Nella Larsen's *Quicksand* and *Passing*. Our goal is to provide access to a wide variety of rare texts. The series includes Fauset's two other novels, *The Chinaberry Tree: A Novel of American Life* and *Comedy: American Style*, and Hurston's short play *Color Struck*, since these are not yet widely available. It also features works by virtually unknown writers, such as *A Tiny Spark*, Christina Moody's slim volume of poetry self-published in 1910, and *Reminiscences of School Life, and Hints on Teaching*, written by Fanny Jackson Coppin in the last year of her life (1913), a multigenre work combining an autobiographical sketch and reflections on trips to England and South Africa, complete with pedagogical advice.

Cultural Studies' investment in diverse resources allows the historic scope of the *African-American Women Writers* series to be more focused than the *Schomburg Library* series, which covered works written over a 137-year period. With few exceptions, the authors included in the *African-American Women Writers* series wrote their major works between 1910 and 1940. The texts reprinted include all the works by each particular author that are not otherwise readily obtainable. As a result, two volumes contain works originally published after 1940. The Charlotte Hawkins Brown volume includes her book of etiquette published in 1941, *The Correct Thing To Do—To Say—To Wear*. One of the poetry volumes contains Maggie Pogue Johnson's *Fallen Blossoms*, published in 1951, a compilation of all her previously published and unpublished poems.

Excavational work by scholars during the past decade has been crucial to the development of *African-American Women Writers, 1910–1940*. Germinal bibliographical sources such as Ann Allen Shockley's *Afro-American Women Writers 1746–1933* and Maryemma Graham's *Database of African-American Women Writers* made the initial identification of texts possible. Other works were brought to our attention by scholars who wrote letters sharing their research. Additional texts by selected authors were then added, so that many volumes contain the complete oeuvres of particular writers. Pieces by authors without enough published work to fill an entire volume were grouped with other pieces by genre.

The two types of collections, those organized by author and those organized by genre, bring out different characteristics of black women's writings of the period. The collected works of the literary writers illustrate that many of them were experimenting with a variety of forms. Mercedes Gilbert's volume, for example, contains her 1931 collection *Selected Gems of Poetry, Comedy, and Drama, Etc.*, as well as her 1938 novel *Aunt Sarah's Wooden God*. Georgia Douglas Johnson's volume contains her plays and short stories in addition to her poetry. Sarah Lee Brown Fleming's volume combines her 1918 novel *Hope's Highway* with her 1920 collection of poetry, *Clouds and Sunshine*.

The generic volumes both bring out the formal and thematic similarities among many of the writings and highlight the striking individuality of particular writers. Most of the plays in the volume of one-acts are social dramas whose tragic endings can be clearly attributed to miscegenation and racism. Within the context of these other plays, Marita Bonner's expressionistic theatrical vision becomes all the more striking.

The volumes of *African-American Women Writers, 1910–1940* contain reproductions of more than one hundred previously published texts, including twenty-nine plays, seventeen poetry collections, twelve novels, six autobiographies, five collections of short biographical sketches, three biographies, three histories of organizations, three black histories, two anthologies, two sociological studies, a diary, and a book of etiquette. Each volume features an introduction by a contemporary scholar that provides crucial biographical data on each author and the historical and critical context of her work. In some cases, little information on the authors was available outside of the fragments of biographical data contained in the original introduction or in the text itself. In these instances, editors have documented the libraries and research centers where they tried to find information, in the hope that subsequent scholars will continue the necessary search to find the "lost" clues to the women's stories in the rich stores of papers, letters, photographs, and other primary materials scattered throughout the country that have yet to be fully catalogued.

Many of the thrilling moments that occurred during the development of this series were the result of previously fragmented pieces of these women's histories suddenly coming together, such as Adele Alexander's uncovering of an old family photograph picturing her own aunt with Addie Hunton, the author Alexander was researching. Claudia Tate's examination of Georgia Douglas Johnson's papers in the Moorland-Spingarn Research Center of Howard University resulted in the discovery of a wealth of previously unpublished work.

The slippery quality of race itself emerged during the construction of the series. One of the short novels originally intended for inclusion in the series had to be cut when the family of the author protested that the writer was not of African descent. Another case involved Louise Kennedy's sociological study *The Negro Peasant Turns Inward*. The fact that none of the available biographical material on Kennedy specifically mentioned race, combined with some coded criticism in a review in the *Crisis*, convinced editor Sheila Smith McKoy that Kennedy was probably white.

These women, taken together, began to chart the true vitality, and complexity, of the literary tradition that African-American women have generated, using a wide variety of forms. They testify to the fact that the monumental works of Hurston, Larsen, and Fauset, for example, emerged out of a larger cultural context; they were not exceptions or aberrations. Indeed, their contributions to American literature and culture, as this series makes clear, were fundamental not only to the shaping of the African-American tradition but to the American tradition as well.

Henry Louis Gates, Jr.
Jennifer Burton

PUBLISHER'S NOTE

In the *African-American Women Writers, 1910–1940* series, G. K. Hall not only is making available previously neglected works that in many cases have been long out of print, we are also, whenever possible, publishing these works in facsimiles reprinted from their original editions including, when available, reproductions of original title pages, copyright pages, and photographs.

When it was not possible for us to reproduce a complete facsimile edition of a particular work (for example, if the original exists only as a handwritten draft or is too fragile to be reproduced), we have attempted to preserve the essence of the original by resetting the work exactly as it originally appeared. Therefore, any typographical errors, strikeouts, or other anomalies reflect our efforts to give the reader a true sense of the original work.

We trust that these facsimile and reprint editions, together with the new introductory essays, will be both useful and historically enlightening to scholars and students alike.

ACKNOWLEDGMENTS

For his continued generosity, Henry Louis Gates, Jr., has my gratitude. For her careful reading of the manuscript, I am in debt to Jennifer Burton. And for their love and support, as always, András Boelcskevy and our children Anna and Steve.

INTRODUCTION

PROFESSION, CALLING, PASTIME: THREE WOMEN POETS

BY MARY ANNE STEWART BOELCSKEVY

The founding moment of African-American literature was a young girl's poem: Lucy Terry's "Bars Fight, August 28, 1746." Her ballad, which recounts the massacre of two families in Deerfield, Massachusetts, by sixty Native Americans, stands with Phillis Wheatley's 1773 collection of poetry, *Poems on Various Subjects, Religious and Moral*, as the beginnings of a literary tradition that has only in the past few decades received widespread critical scholarly attention.[1] Although anthologies published in the 1980s brought many hitherto neglected women authors back into print and to critical attention, volumes on the women's tradition of African-American literature have concentrated on the prose rather than the poetry.[2] The reprinting of nineteenth- and twentieth-century women poets provides a larger context for the important scholarly work on the African-American women's tradition in poetry already begun.[3] Much work still lies ahead.

The volumes of poetry by Clara Ann Thompson, J. Pauline Smith, and Mazie Earhart Clark reprinted here were originally published in Cincinnati and Detroit in the decade between 1922 and 1932, the years of the Harlem Renaissance. In *Shadowed Dreams: Women's Poetry of the Harlem Renaissance*, Maureen Honey writes that "the peculiar blend of romanticism, hedonism, anger and faith in the capacity of art to effect change marks the twenties as a special time."[4] Thompson, Smith, and Clark were not among the literati gathered in Harlem, however; they remained close to home while they wrote their poems. Even though their concerns are not those of the Harlem poets, these three poets explore key elements of their early-twentieth-century world: technological advances, world war, and economic depression; club women, church work, and racial uplift; piety, humor, and popular romance. In what was still imagined as the "Woman's Century," each of these women had a different concept of herself as poet. Poetry was a profession for Thompson; a calling for Smith; and a pastime for Clark. From Detroit and Cincinnati, Clara Ann Thompson's 1926 *A Garland of Poems*, J. Pauline Smith's 1922 *"Exceeding Riches" and Other Verse*, and Mazie Earhart Clark's 1932 *Garden of Memories* form a bridge between an earlier poetry and that of the Harlem Renaissance and provide a challenge to our ongoing critical assessment of the African-American women's tradition in poetry.

CLARA ANN THOMPSON[5]
(1869?–1949)
A GARLAND OF POEMS (1926)

Clara Ann Thompson is the best known of these three poets. Born in Rossmoyne, Ohio, she was the daughter of John Henry and Clara Jane (Gray) Thompson, former Virginia slaves. Birth dates for Thompson vary from source to source.[6] She was educated in Rossmoyne public schools and tutored privately. Trained to be a teacher, she abandoned the profession after one year to concentrate on writing, elocution, and public readings of her own work.[7] Thompson was a member of the YWCA, the NAACP, and the Baptist Church; she did social work and taught catechism at St. Andrew Episcopal Church in Cincinnati.[8]

Two of Thompson's five siblings—her brother Aaron Belford Thompson and her sister Priscilla Jane Thompson—were also published poets.[9] According to *Who's Who in Colored America*, Clara Ann Thompson's publications included *Songs from the Wayside* (self-published, 1908);[10] "What Means This Bleating?" (self-published, 1921; second edition, 1923); "There Came Wise Men" (self-published, 1923); and *A Garland of Poems* (Boston: Christopher Publishing, 1926). Wendell Phillips Dabney notes that Thompson "received requests from anthologists to use her poems, among them Carl Kjersmeier, a Danish anthologist, who praised her poems very highly."[11]

Of the three poets reprinted here, Thompson has also received the most critical attention. In *An Anthology of Verse by American Negroes* (1924), Walter Clinton Jackson and Newman Ivey White anthologized "His Answer" and "Mrs. Johnson Objects" from *Songs from the Wayside*; in White's "Bibliographical and Critical Notes" to the anthology, he compares Clara Ann favorably to her brother and sister, praising her for better "artistic finish" and for exercising "more restraint," but concludes that she "has no breadth of view, or intensity or much imagination, and not much culture."[12] Joan Sherman mentions Thompson in an essay on her brother, Aaron Belford Thompson, in *Invisible Poets* (1974); in her longer assessment of Thompson in *Collected Black Women's Poetry* (1988), Sherman considers Thompson's "output . . . noteworthy only in its quantity," finding the three dialect poems featuring Uncle Rube to have "more 'flavor' than all the other thirty-three verses in *Songs*."[13] Erlene Stetson includes Thompson in *Black Sister* under "Eighteenth- and Nineteenth-Century Poets" and reprints "His Answer" and "Mrs. Johnson Objects." Ann Allen Shockley selects "Uncle Rube on the Race Problem" for her anthology, *Afro-American Women Writers, 1746–1933*.[14] She notes that although Thompson's work appeared in anthologies, it was "not generally admired."[15] Clara Ann Thompson and Priscilla Jane Thompson are considered in the same entry in *The Feminist Companion to Literature in English* by Blain, Clements, and Grundy, who also single out for praise Clara Ann's creation of the "ironic, humorous political commentator," Uncle Rube. More recently, Roses and Randolph argue that "Thompson's poems deserve an attention they have never received" and suggest that the poems be placed "in the broader context of Afro-American and women's literary history."[16]

Thompson's wish was to be a novelist, but, as she explains in her foreword to *A Garland of Poems*, "the writing of poetry has been thrust upon me." The would-be novelist's ability to create characters and her use of dialogue are more impressive than her poetry at times, especially in her dialect poems. Uncle Rube makes another appearance in "Uncle Rube on Church Quarrels," the first of the fifty-five poems in *A Garland of Poems*. Uncle Rube takes the churches— "Baptist, Methodist an' Christian"(11)—to task for forgetting their mission to save souls in their fighting among themselves, harboring "triflin' preacher[s]"(12) and "shieldin' membahs"(14). In "Aunt Mandy's Grandchildren," Thompson makes good use of dialect to represent generational differences as well. A younger woman listens to Aunt Mandy, who is convinced that "Dah's a spell on all Nell's children"(60), but offers her own view that spoiling rather than conjuration is to blame. Thompson's narrator displays a generosity of spirit toward "poor old fashioned, love blind granny"(61) by recognizing her need to keep her old beliefs. Other poems using dialect include "Showin' Off," "Pap's Advice," "Goin' to Foot It All the Way (Aunt Betty Testifies)," and "Circumstantial Evidence."

Unlike Smith and Clark, Thompson writes explicitly about race, and incorporates a variety of perspectives. In "What Means This Bleating of the Sheep?" Thompson castigates America, "proud freedom's land, / Thy flag is trailing in the dust!"(78). She traces the country's history of denying freedom to African-Americans from the beginning of slavery, noting that an opportunity for redemption was missed: Emancipation came not "Because they hated slavery, / But that their fair united land, / Might ever undivided be (79)." She exhorts the country to rid itself of the mob and the Ku Klux Klan, and warns that it will suffer the consequences of God's wrath if it does not do so. In the final stanzas, Thompson warns that America would do better to help "the loyal African"(82) than to court the anarchy arriving from foreign shores. Published twice, in 1921 and in 1923, this poem shifts in its treatment of political expediency. For most of the poem, Thompson's stance is that America will feel God's wrath in part because it made a political rather than an ethical decision to end slavery. The continuation of racism is the sign that nothing has changed. In the closing stanzas, however, Thompson draws upon the "red scare" mentality of the twenties to contrast the African-American and the anarchist-foreigner, using the political expediency of "othering" well to highlight "Americanness."

That "Our Side of the Race Problem" follows this poem immediately speaks to Thompson's desire, as she puts it in the foreword, "to present both sides of the subject, knowing that no problem can be truly solved in any other way"([9]). Here Thompson focuses on the divisiveness within the race. An overly long poem, it loses its focus as its exhortations shift from African-American men in their race and gender relations to ministers in their leadership roles. Thompson speaks to the men of race disloyalty and of their need to stand on their feet and to protect their women, who will "gladly follow" them (88). The lines "How can we rise if none excel? / Where will our leaders be?"(85) allude to W. E. B. Du Bois's concept of the Talented Tenth. Ministers are chastised for their pride and reminded that they are the servants of their flocks. As we read the many stanzas, the poem begins to lose its momentum, yet we can imagine how powerful both of these poems were in their public readings by Thompson, who was known as a "fine elocutionist."

Thompson's advice poems in *A Garland of Poems* tend to speak to middle-class aspirations. "Showin' Off" condemns materialism but also reacts to loudness as an offense to decorum—"'Case you know de unfair white folks— / Put us all into one boat"(23). "Be True to the Best" advises "patient, sincere cultivation / Of all that is pure in the heart"(26). Thompson tells the pupils watching the dedication of "The New Schoolhouse" at Mount Healthy, Ohio, "And dream your bright dreams, for bright dreams are your due; / But remember 'tis work that makes them come true"(36) "Pap's Advice," "The Flirt," and "Faint Heart" use lighter verse to offer advice to lovers—the first two with good humor. Thompson's social work is alluded to in "The Settlement Worker's Prayer" and in the closing stanza of "The Mothers Dear":

> And while with grateful homage
> The mothers' praise we sing,
> Let's breathe a prayer for that one
> Who has no wedding ring.
>
> (68)

Thompson's occasional verses include "Life and Death," written in memory of Booker T. Washington; as well as "Our Deceased

Leader" and "'I Have Lived For This Hour'" written for local church workers. "Raymond G. Dandridge" praises Cincinnati's "invalid poet." In "More Than Ninety Years," Thompson pays tribute to those who founded Cincinnati's Union Baptist Church in 1831:

> They dared to do what colored men
> Of weaker courage dared not do—
> They strove to be intelligent,
> And still unto their God be true.
>
> (69)

Two other poems, "Our Soldiers" and "Our Heroes," celebrate, respectively, the departure and the return of Cincinnati's World War I "colored troops." "Easter 1919" remembers those killed not only in the war but in the worldwide influenza epidemic that began in 1918. There are several religious poems and a few nature poems in the collection; these are, for the most part, unremarkable.

While religious and sentimental poetry can often be dismissed by modern readers, such verses spoke to the needs of the times. World war abroad and domestic war waged by the Klan had taken their toll, and the influenza epidemic had left 22 million dead worldwide by 1920. Religious poetry reflects the search for comfort in the aftermath of so many deaths due to "war and pestilence." Moreover, in the pre–New Deal era, the church's role was not limited to spiritual life; its educational and social work was of central importance to the African-American community. As efforts are made to place Thompson's poetry in what Roses and Randolph call "the broader context of Afro-American and women's literary history"[17] and attention paid to the conservatism of much late-nineteenth- and early-twentieth-century African-American poetry, the question of generational differences also takes on significance. Clara Ann and her siblings were the children of ex-slaves. How the unique pressure on such children to succeed may have influenced them to make cautious choices remains to be examined.

J. PAULINE SMITH[18]
(??–??)
"EXCEEDING RICHES" AND OTHER VERSE (1922)

Unlike Clara Ann Thompson, J. Pauline Smith did not consider poetry her profession; for her, it was a calling. A native of Windsor, Ontario, J. Pauline Smith lived from early childhood in Detroit, Michigan. According to a 1915 publication entitled *Michigan Manual of Freedmen's Progress*,[19] as a young girl Smith was so intrigued by the symbols of stenography that she taught herself the skill and began to practice it by reporting sermons and lectures. Later she studied typewriting at a business college. She was unable to find employment for several years, until she managed to set up desk space at the African-American law firm of Barnes and Stowers in Detroit as a public stenographer. By 1914 Smith had enough business to open her own office in the Chamber of Commerce Building. For a short time, Smith also served as the official stenographer of the Michigan Freedmen's Progress Commission, but left that temporary job to carry on her own business. She was a dedicated church worker at the Bethel A. M. E. Church.

Before the 1922 publication of *"Exceeding Riches" and Other Verse*, Smith had published her verse in numerous periodicals[20] and in a 1917 gift booklet, "The Heart of Christmas." She was also the compiler of the 1903 publication, *Olive Prints*, a collection of quotations from Robert Browning's poetry.[21] The foreword to *"Exceeding Riches"* was written by Theresa Smith, a fellow Windsor, Ontario, transplant to Detroit. A professor of English and general historian,[22] Theresa Smith sees these verses as supplying the need of a postwar world for "things of the spirit" and compares their author—who "triumphs over every vicissitude of fortune because her mind is fixed upon the eternal"—to Wordsworth and Milton (vii/[103]).

J. Pauline Smith dedicates her book to her mother, "whose lullaby songs were all from the Methodist Church Hymnal"([99]). Not surprisingly, the majority of Smith's poems are religious, some echoing the common measure and long measure of those hymns.

The book's title poem, "Exceeding Riches," is a meditation on verses from Paul's Epistle to the Ephesians: "That in the coming ages he might show the exceeding riches of his grace in kindness toward us in Christ Jesus. For by my grace you have been saved through faith, and this is not your own doing it is the gift of God."[23] Paul's influence on his namesake is shown in her poem "A Name":

> So well he wrote and with such power,
>> Such logic, clear and keen,
> Men call the epistles from his pen
>> Of very right—"Pauline."
>
> They breathe the spirit of a man
>> Who, counting not the price,
> So loved and served that he could say,
>> "For me to live is Christ."
>
> In after years how it must thrill
>> And mould the life, I ween,
> When parents o'er baptismal vows
>> Have named a child—"Pauline."
>>> (37/[133])

"Paul" is the name used by the man called Saul after his conversion. Smith's use of an initial before the name "Pauline" highlights the connection she felt to Paul and is perhaps a sign of her own faith.[24]

"Exceeding Riches" and Other Verse is divided into three sections: "Meditations" (fifty poems), "Festival Days" (fifteen poems), and "Miscellaneous" (fifteen poems and a final repetition of "When the Heart Keeps Christmas," from the previous section). The first two sections contain religious poems exclusively. Some of the poems—"Three Things," "'That Bread of Life,'" "Is Your Name Ahisamach?"—were inspired by sermons or by Bible lessons at the Detroit YWCA. "'No More Sea'" was written in response to a poem in the *Literary Digest*. The "Festival Days" section reprints verses previously printed in Smith's gift booklet, "The Heart of

Christmas." The "Miscellaneous" section contains primarily occasional verse, much of it religious.

Twenty-two of Smith's poems—all but one located in the "Meditations" section—cite specific verses of Scripture. Eleven of these verses are from the Old Testament, eleven from the New Testament. Four meditations—"'He That Keepeth Israel,'" "'Pleasures Forevermore,'" "The Universal Call," and "God's Secret"—are from Psalms; four others—"'Exceeding Riches,'" "'Though Our Outward Man Perish,'" "'That I May Know Him,'" and "'Those Things Which Are Before'"—are from the Epistles of Paul. These meditations tend to recast the message of the verse into poetic form, but in a few instances, the verse is just a starting place. Smith takes the question in Matthew 5:47—"And if you salute only your brethren, what more are you doing than others?"—as an occasion to praise the "more than others" people who "keep the world aglow." In "Exceeding Riches," she intertwines two lines from the hymn "Amazing Grace" in its stanzas— "I once was blind, but now I see" and "But shall not know till face to face"—with the different rhythm of her own lines in echo and resistance to that other hymn (15/[111]). In "The Universal Call," Psalm 50:1, the line "The mighty God the Lord speaks and summons the earth from the rising of the sun to its setting" is played out over a twentieth-century landscape where the call of God is "More swift than wireless thro' the air" (46/[142]). The fifty poems in the "Meditations" section are testaments of Christian faith, hope, and charity.

The fifteen poems of "Festival Days" are arranged to span the year. The three New Year's poems are fairly uninspired. Six poems celebrate Easter with a variety of rhyme and form. "The Message of Easter," for example, makes use of internal rhyme to create trinities of rhyme within its quatrains: tomb–gloom–illume, word–stirred–heard, calls–falls–enthralls, broken–token–spoken, o'er–before–shore, and light–might–night. Two poems mark Thanksgiving in religious and patriotic tones: "God's ancient covenant with earth" (68/[164]) and "our whole great nation's strength" (69/[165]). The "Festival Days" section closes with four Christmas poems. In its warning that we not "[miss] the chant, the sight sublime," "The Heart of Christmas" uses images drawn from contemporary life: "The auto's noisy puff and gong" and "Christmas bargains cheap and rare"(70/[166])

Occasional verse, praise, and nature poems make up the fifteen selections of poetry in the final ("Miscellaneous") section of *"Exceeding Riches."* The centenary of Robert Browning's birth, the fiftieth anniversary of the YWCA, the centennial of the founding by Richard Allen of the African Methodist Episcopal Church, the tercentenary of the settlement of the country, the eightieth anniversary of Detroit's Bethel A. M. E. Church, and even the birthday ("one hundred and odd years") of the American flag are celebrated in lyric verse, some meant to be sung to well-known tunes. The work of both the club woman and the Red Cross worker garner praise. Two poems confront war. A few nature poems also appear in this section, of which "Robin Redbreast," written for a child, is the best. One poem ends with the cryptic caution, "Lest injury should hap to souls, / Heed: 'School, drive slowly'"(84/[180]).

Christian faith is Smith's primary theme. Race is mentioned in only a few poems and then quite subtly. "A Prayer" begins "Use me, Lord, use me for my race, / To send their status up a pace; / To make their merits better known; / Hasten their coming to their own!"(54/[150]). But the repetition of the first line with the substitution of "Thy Church" and "Thyself alone" in the subsequent two quatrains sets up a climax in which race is of the least concern. "Kinship with Christ" gives the best sense of Smith's priorities; that is, that our kinship with the King of Kings outweighs any earthly distinctions. As with race, war may be the subject, but religion is the answer in Smith's three "war poems." The first, "A Prayer for the Times—1914," is international in scope, speaking of "these days of war's array"(20/[116]) in reference to World War I, which was then beginning in Europe. "A War-Time Prayer—1917" marks the entry of the United States into the war, asking God to "guard our soldiers" and to "Let democracy's triumph, distinctions efface, / All men be brothers, regardless of race!"(88/[184]). Her final "war poem" is a meditation on the cause of war, based on James 4:1.

Females are the subject of five poems. "Is Your Name Ahisamach?," "The Club Woman," and "Y.W.C.A. Anniversary Song" celebrate sisterhood and the important social services women provide. "Lost—Our Little Girls" bemoans a perceived breakdown in gender distinction in clothing: "Which is Sally, which is Jim?" and pleads with "Dame Fashion" to "Give us back our little girls!"(85/[181]). The women around Christ are the subject of "The First Easter Morning."

> I'm glad that women linger'd longest
> Where "they crucified Him."
> I'm glad their love was true and strongest
> That they ne'er denied Him!
>
> I'm glad that three of them were first
> At day's faint dawning,
> To find that He death's chains had burst
> On earth's first Easter morning!
>
> I'm glad it was a woman's name
> Held His first greeting;
> When Mary to the garden came—
> Oh, that wondrous meeting!
> (67/[163])

Here, Smith combines her faith with a distinctly feminist pride.

Smith shows formal skill in her verse, favoring couplets and quatrains. "'Not Otherwise,'" a parable in which a minister on a visit to a sick woman realizes that "Hers was the ministry that day"(49/[145]), is a narrative poem composed of three long stanzas of couplets ending in a tercet formed by the refrain "I would not have it otherwise." The brevity and tone of the four-line poem "Omnipotence" is reminiscent of Emily Dickinson's verses:

> A whole Red Sea
> Is quite impassable to you and me;
> But God's power at man's impossible starts,
> And, lo, each Red Sea He divides in parts!
> (53/[149])

In "Robin Redbreast," Smith alternates tercets and couplets to mimic a robin as he pauses briefly on the garden fence.

For J. Pauline Smith, poetry was an expression of her deep Christian faith. In her piety and attention to religious subjects, Smith may seem to share more with her eighteenth- and nineteenth-century predecessors than with her twentieth-century successors. Phillis Wheatley's collection of verse was, after all, *Poems on Various Subjects, Religious and Moral.* Furthermore, as James Weldon Johnson noted in his preface to *The Book of American Negro Poetry*, Thomas Jefferson's famous criticism—"Religion has produced a Phillis Wheatley, but it could not produce a poet"—"was directed more against religion than Phillis' poetry."[25] Religious poetry poses a particular challenge. Feminist scholarship suggests that women in order to speak often borrowed the authority of religion, Christianity in particular. Religious poetry is not an artifact of the eighteenth and nineteenth centuries, however. As Jane Hirshfield points out in *Women in Praise of the Sacred: Forty-three Centuries of Spiritual Poetry by Women*, there is a long-standing, international women's tradition of spiritual poetry. It is a tradition to which both Wheatley and Smith might lay claim.

MAZIE EARHART CLARK[26]
(1874–1958)
GARDEN OF MEMORIES (1932)

While poetry may have been a profession for the would-be novelist Thompson and a calling for the stenographer J. Pauline Smith, for Mazie Earhart Clark it was a pastime. Born in 1874 in Glendale, Hamilton County, Ohio, Mazie Earhart Clark was the daughter of David and Fanny Earhart. Her mother died when she was five. Her early education was in the Glendale public schools. Clark later went to Cincinnati to study chiropody (what we now call podiatry). Wendell Phillips Dabney writes that, around 1906, Clark—under the name Mrs. Mazie Earhart—"opened a first class establishment . . . in connection with a 'shoppe' of beauty culture." He also calls her "a writer of songs, author of creditable poems."[27] Clark was a member of the Union Baptist Church. Her husband, George J. Clark, a U.S. Army sergeant, died in 1919.[28]

Clark's poems appeared in many periodicals. *Garden of Memories*, reprinted here, may not be her first book of poetry. The Library of Congress lists a 1917 publication, *Life's Pathway: Little Lyrics of Love, Loyalty and Devotion* (Cincinnati: Press of S. C. Higbee), authored by Mazie Angela Earhart. However, a survey of available biographical information on Clark did not yield a middle name for her.[29] It is possible that Clark's poetry writing may have been interrupted by the death of her husband in 1919. In the foreword to *Garden of Memories*, which appeared thirteen years later, in 1932, Clark writes, "After his passing, it was as though I had reached the cross-roads in life,—I seemed to have run up a blind alley, where one cannot see what lies head [*sic*], and is afraid to go on"([5]/[189]). Whether or not the earlier work is hers, Clark did write a subsequent work in 1940, *Life's Sunshine and Shadows*, which was published, as was *Garden of Memories*, by Eaton Publishing Company in Cincinnati. Only the poems on the first forty-eight pages of *Life's Sunshine and Shadows* are new; the rest repeat exactly those in *Garden of Memories*.[30]

Clark offers the poems in *Garden of Memories*, as she explains in her foreword, "in the hope and belief that . . . [they] may prove comforting and stimulating"([5]/[189]). The poems do not treat any particular racial themes but speak to a larger popular American culture. Of the more than eighty poems, almost half take nature or romance as their themes, and many are reminiscent of popular romantic songs of the time, with moonlit paths, roses, and absent lovers abounding. Another twenty have religious themes; five others urge acceptance of fate. Clark has ten poems that could be classified as narratives, as well as four elegies and four dialect poems. "My Southern Home" and "My Home in Virginia," about Mississippi and Virginia respectively, could be classified as plantation poems, although the latter focuses more on mother than on home. Mother's Day had been proclaimed a national holiday by President Woodrow Wilson in 1914, and Clark's "A Tribute to Mother" was written to celebrate the holiday. Other tributes to motherhood are "Mother Always Understands," "Mother," and, for her own mother, "Guardian Angel."

Many of Clark's poems, light as they may be, give us a glimpse of the world of the 1920s. Radio was to the twenties what cyberspace is to the nineties: a new mode of communication. Newspapers ran radio columns to report on the latest news and to answer consumer questions about the new technology. In its April 18, 1922, edition, *The Detroit News* in its "Radio Department" column reported, under the headline "Enter radio, in the role of Cupid," that "radio is destined to become the master of matchmakers." Thus, in "Her Lost Valentine," Clark urges Dan Cupid to "Call the broadcasting station / Get on the line, / Send out a message / To her lost valentine"([16]/[200]). Working with everyday things, Clark's "The Christmas Tree" speaks of the presents that might be found underneath the family tree: "There are skates and a wagon / For Willie and Joe, / A doll and a buggy / For Lula and Flo. / Father some handkerchiefs / With dotes in the corner, / Bob a story book / About Jack Horner"([34]/[218]). To record the everyday banalities, even without higher purpose, is to write a kind of social history. Thus, the poem "The Circus," written during Prohibition, vividly sets the parade scene, complete with ". . . vendors of peanuts and lemonade, / And bootleggers selling home brew"([40]/[224]). For Clark, bootlegging is part of a commonplace scene rather than a historic event, so her circus parade ends with the requisite rainstorm. At the root of the resignation of "The Coming of Old Age" we can find not Christianity but Social Darwinism: "So now's the time to step aside / Let youth take your place, / Boys you know must have their fling / And you have run your race"([21]/[205]). It is not a sentiment that Clark voices very often in her poetry, but it is echoed in "The Hands of Fate," where she writes "Tho' the forces change / It would be too late / The chain has been forged / And welded by fate"([51]/[235]).

More often, Clark's verses are light romantic musings or religious celebrations. Poems like "Are You Lonesome?," "My Dear Old Honey Moon," and "Beautiful Moonbeams" call to mind songs popular in American culture at the time: Bob Cole and Rosamond Johnson's "Lazy Moon" (c. 1903), Irving Berlin's "What'll I Do?" (1924), and Bert Kalmar and Harry Ruby's "Nevertheless" (1931). Religious poems form a large part of Clark's collection. The Christmas season is recognized with "Hosanna in the Highest" and "Christmas Chimes," Easter with "Let's Glorify Him" and "Christ the Lord Is Risen." Creation is the theme of "Common Clay or Adam and Eve" and "God's Gift to Mankind." Salvation is the subject of "When I Get Over There," "My Prayer," "Jesus Is Mine," "Spiritual Birth," and "On Calvary's Brow." "Vespers" praises the inspirational power of music, as played by church organist Mrs. Ann Howard Matthews.

When Clark deals explicitly with current events, as she does in five poems, her focus is on universal themes. Clark commemorates "our dear soldier boys" of World War I in patriotic and religious tones in "Unfurl the Flag" and "Armistice Day." She celebrates Charles Lindbergh's solo flight from New York to Paris on May 20, 1927, in "'Lindy' (America's Boy)." In the sentimental "Baby's Kisses," Clark mourns the 1932 kidnapping and murder of the Lindbergh baby. The daily tribulations of Depression-era life are surveyed in "Brotherhood of Mankind." Perhaps the strongest poem of the five, it uses narrative to evoke the conditions of the family man looking for work and the assistance offered by the "Brotherhood of Mankind."

> His dear ones wait and wonder
> > Why he does not bring them food,
> He walks the street, bemoans his fate,
> > In a sad and mournful mood.
> As he walks, he scans each face,
> > Some young, but lined with care,
> Others happy, heedless, selfish,
> > Would not of their abundance share.
>
> ([14]/[198])

Clark's strong narrative sense is also evident in three other long poems. "The Vision" tells the story of an artist's model whose life is changed after she poses as the Madonna beside a sacred rose bush. In "The Call of an Indian Maid," Shooting Star answers his beloved's call and deserts his school in the East: "He declared civilization a bother / Traded his books / For fish lines and hooks / And returned to the land of his father"([52]/[236]). The most polished of the three, "An Ancient Love Story," retells in couplets the story "told in Babylon / A city of ancient and great renown" of lovers parted when "the prince of noble birth" must "fight as his ancestors did"([57]/[241]).

Although it is a garden Clark offers us in the collection's title, her nature poems are her weakest. Imagery tends to be either conventional or vague. The "many colored lights / Dropping from the trees" ([17]/[201]) of "Autumn Leaves" or the invitation to "inhale the sweet perfume / Exuding from the flowers, / Radiant in their bloom"([58]/[242]) of "Come Walk among the Flowers" are examples of Clark at her most uninspired.

The four penultimate selections in *Garden of Memories* are dialect poems: "The Race-Track Romance," "The Envious Neighbor," "Harvest Time," and "Mammy Knows." Although all four are conventional in terms of subject matter, the first two make good use of Clark's strong narrative sense and a particularly feminine kind of humor. In "The Race Track Romance," the wife of George Washington Brown narrates the evening her husband's racetrack days come to an end, in a dramatic monologue complete with asides to the audience. When Miss Malinda Slack shows up at the Brown home, the narrator tells us in an aside, "(Dat woman didn't spec' to fin' me hyar)"([59]/[243]) as she invites her in. The narrator compliments—in a left-handed, feminine fashion—Malinda's new dress: "I think it gran' an' lubly, / But jist a little tight across de ches'"([59]/[243]). The wife intercepts the note Malinda passes to George Washington Brown, reads it, and the jig is up: "Malinda callin' him baby names, / Telling him she was awfully blue, / An' she would jist haf to seed him / (Her baby)   (Aside) / For jist a little while"([60]/[244]). In another poem, "The Envious Neighbor," a small-town woman—sister, perhaps, to the porch-sitting women in Zora Neale Hurston's *Their Eyes Were Watching God*—sits passing judgment on "old Sister Ruggie": "I ain't sayin' dat she flirts, / I'se just tellin' you' how it 'pears"([61]/[245]).

The more than eighty poems collected in Mazie Earhart Clark's *Garden of Memories* do not lay claim to the title of great art. They were offered as comfort and stimulation to her contemporaries, women who, like herself, had lost a loved one; who worked for a living; and who, in the midst of their American dreams, also believed in moonlight, roses, and romance.

Notes

1.   Lucy Terry's poem was published for the first time in George Sheldon's *A History of Deerfield* (Deerfield: 1985). Phillis Wheatley's book of poems appeared in England in 1773; the American edition was published in 1786.

2.   See especially: Mary Helen Washington, ed., *Black-Eyed Susans: Classic Stories by and about Black Women* (Garden City, N.Y.: Anchor Books, 1975); Ann Allen Shockley, *Afro-American Women Writers 1746–1933: An Anthology and Critical Guide* (New York: Penguin [Meridian], 1988); and Henry Louis Gates, Jr., gen. ed., *The Schomburg Library of Nineteenth-Century Black Women Writers* (New York: Oxford University Press, 1988–   ).

3   Recent work on the women's tradition in poetry includes: Erlene Stetson, *Black Sister: Poetry by Black American Women, 1746–1980* (Bloomington: Indiana University Press, 1981); Gloria Hull, *Color, Sex, and Poetry: Three Women Writers of the Harlem Renaissance* (Bloomington: Indiana University Press, 1987); Joan R. Sherman, ed., *Collected Black Women's Poetry*, vol. in Gates, gen. ed., *The Schomburg Library of Nineteenth-Century Black Women Writers* (New York: Oxford University Press, 1988–   ); Joan R. Sherman, *African-American Poetry of the Nineteenth Century* (Urbana: University of Chicago Press, 1992); and Maureen Honey, *Shadowed Dreams: Women's Poetry of the Harlem Renaissance* (New Brunswick: Rutgers University Press, 1989).

4.   Honey, *Shadowed Dreams*, 1.

5.   Biographical sources for Clara Ann Thompson include: Shockley, *Afro-American Women Writers*; Sherman, ed., *African-American Poetry*; Stetson, *Black Sister*; William Coyle, *Ohio Authors and Their Books* (Cleveland: World Publishing Company, 1962); Wendell Phillips Dabney, *Cincinnati's Colored Citizens* (Cincinnati: 1926); *Who's Who in Colored America*, vols. 1928–29; 1930–32; 1933–37; 1938–40; and 1941–44 (New York: Christian E. Burckel); Newman Ivey White and Walter Clinton Jackson, *An Anthology of Verse by American Negroes* (Durham, N.C.: 1924); Lorraine Elena Roses and Ruth Elizabeth Randolph, *Harlem Renaissance and Beyond* (Boston: G. K. Hall, 1990); Theresa Gunnels Rush, Carol Fairbanks Myers, and Esther Spring Arata,

Black American Writers Past and Present: A Biographical and Bibliographical Dictionary (Metuchen, N.J.: Scarecrow, 1975); Virginia Blain, Patricia Clements, and Isobel Grundy, *The Feminist Companion to Literature in English: Women Writers from the Middle Ages to the Present* (New Haven: Yale University Press, 1990).

6. Joan Sherman, in *Invisible Poets: Afro-Americans of the Nineteenth Century* (Urbana: University of Illinois Press, 1974; 2nd. ed., 1989), estimates a birth date of 1887 for her, based on portraits that appear in volumes of poetry published by Thompson and her siblings. Shockley gives 1869, based on the estimate that Thompson died at age eighty, given in the *Cincinnati Enquirer*'s 1949 obituary for her. The date 1869 is used by Roses and Randolph as well as by Blain et al.

7. Dabney, *Cincinnati's Colored Citizens*, 320.

8. Shockley, *Afro-American Women Writers*, 321; Dabney, *Cincinnati's Colored Citizens*, 320.

9. Thompson's other three siblings were Garland Yancey, to whom Thompson dedicates *A Garland of Poems*; a third brother who, according to the opening poem in *Songs from the Wayside*, "To My Dead Brother," died when Thompson was young; and a sister whose death two years after her mother's death is mentioned in "She Prayed."

10 *Songs from the Wayside* was reprinted in Sherman, *Black Women's Poetry*.

11. Dabney, *Cincinnati's Colored Citizens*, 320.

12. White and Jackson, *An Anthology of Verse by American Negroes*, 233.

13. The poems in *A Garland of Poems*, Sherman writes, are "fifty-five musings on religious, moral, romantic, and race topics that are much like those of 1908" (*Schomburg*, xxxiv).

14. "Uncle Rube on the Race Problem," "His Answer," and "Mrs. Johnson Objects" were three of the seven poems White originally singled out in his critical notes on *Songs from the Wayside*. Shockley's repetition of this earlier judgment of worth is an interesting phenomenon—one that also demonstrates how, as critical reception shifts, a poem comes to represent quite different concerns. Thus, "Uncle Rube on the Race Problem" can be considered variously as an example of dialect, race issues, generational representations, subversion, dialogics, and signifying.

15. Shockley, *Afro-American Women Writers*, 281.

16. Roses and Randolph, *Harlem Renaissance and Beyond*, 314.

17. Roses and Randolph, *Harlem Renaissance and Beyond*, 314.

18.   No dates could be found for Smith. The primary biographical source for Smith is *The Michigan Manual of Freedmen's Progress*; Roses and Randolph also include biographical information on Smith.

19.   J. Pauline Smith is featured on pp. 59–60 in the chapter entitled "Afro Americans Engaged in Professional Pursuits," in Michigan Freedmen's Progress Commission, *Michigan Manual of Freedman's Progress*, compiled by Francis H. Warren (Detroit: Michigan Freedman's Progress Commission, 1915).

20.   The "magazines, religious and secular papers" Smith cites in her preface include a YWCA publication entitled "Detroit Young Women," as well as "Detroit Club Woman," *Detroit Leader, Detroit Free Press*, and the Philadelphia-based *Christian Recorder*.

21.   Smith's admiration of Browning—common to many at this time—can also be seen in her poem "Robert Browning," written on the centennial of his birth and included in *"Exceeding Riches."*

22.   *Michigan Manual* lists both J. Pauline Smith and Theresa Smith. Although they both are native to Windsor and Theresa lives in Detroit "with her mother and sister," no relation to J. Pauline is mentioned.

23.   Ephesians 2:7–8. All Bible quotations are from Herbert G. May and Bruce M. Metzger, eds., *The Oxford Annotated Bible*, rev. standard ed. (New York: Oxford University Press, 1965).

24.   No records were found stating what the initial "J" stood for in Smith's name.

25.   Introduction to James Weldon Johnson, ed., *The Book of American Negro Poetry* (New York: Harcourt Brace and Company, 1922, xxiii; rev. ed. New York: Harcourt Brace Jovanovich, 1983).

26.   Biographical sources for Clark include: William Coyle, ed., *Ohio Authors and Their Books: Biographies for Ohio Authors, Native and Resident, 1796–1950* (Cleveland: World Publishing Company, 1962); Theresa Gunnels, Carol Fairbanks Myers, and Esther Spring Arata, *Black American Writers Past and Present: A Biographical and Bibliographical Dictionary* (Metuchen, N.J.: Scarecrow, 1975); and Roses and Randolph, *Harlem Renaissance and Beyond*.

27.   Dabney, *Cincinnati's Colored Citizens*, 269.

28.   Roses and Randolph note that Clark's husband was buried in Arlington Cemetery (54).

29.   In *The Bibliographical Guide to African-American Women Writers* (Westport, Conn.: Greenwood Press, 1993), Casper Leroy Jordan, compiler, lists a partial title of this work under Mazie Earhart Clark, but with a 1935 publication by Eaton.

30.   In Roses and Randolph, *Harlem Renaissance and Beyond*, 54–55.

Bibliography

PRIMARY SOURCES

Clark, Mazie Earhart. *Garden of Memories*. Cincinnati: Eaton Publishing Company, 1932.

———. *Life's Sunshine and Shadows*. Cincinnati: Eaton Publishing Company, 1940.

Earhart, Mazie Angela. *Life's Pathway: Little Lyrics of Love, Loyalty and Devotion*. Cincinnati: Press of S. C. Higbee, 1917. (Attribution of this book to Mazie Earhart Clark has not been confirmed.)

Smith, J. Pauline. *"Exceeding Riches" and Other Verse*. Detroit: 1922.

———. *Olive Prints: Selections from Robert Browning's Poems for Every Day in the Year*. Detroit: Press of W. Graham, 1903.

Thompson, Clara Ann. *A Garland of Poems*. Boston: Christopher Publishing House, 1926.

———. *Songs from the Wayside*. Rossmoyne, Ohio: author, 1908.

SECONDARY SOURCES

Blain, Virginia, Patricia Clements, and Isobel Grundy. *The Feminist Companion to Literature in English: Women Writers from the Middle Ages to the Present*. New Haven: Yale University Press, 1990.

Bontemps, Arna. *American Negro Poetry: Revised Edition*. New York: Hill and Wang, 1974.

Brown, Sterling. *"Negro Poetry and Drama" and "The Negro in American Fiction."* New York: Atheneum, 1969 (originally published 1937).

Coyle, William, ed. *Ohio Authors and Their Books: Biographical Data and Selective Bibliographies for Ohio Authors, Native and Resident, 1796–1950*. Cleveland: World Publishing Company, 1962.

Dabney, Wendell Phillips. *Cincinnati's Colored Citizens*. Cincinnati, 1926.

Gates, Henry Louis, Jr., ed. *The Schomburg Library of Nineteenth-Century Black Women Writers*, 30 volumes. New York: Oxford University Press, 1988– .

Hirshfield, Jane, ed. *Women in Praise of the Sacred: Forty-three Centuries of Spiritual Poetry by Women*. New York: HarperCollins, 1994.

Honey, Maureen. *Shadowed Dreams: Women's Poetry of the Harlem Renaissance*. New Brunswick: Rutgers University Press, 1989.

Hughes, Langston, and Arna Bontemps, eds. *The Poetry of the Negro, 1746–1970*. Garden City, N.Y.: Doubleday and Company, 1970.

Hull, Gloria. *Color, Sex and Poetry: Three Women Writers of the Harlem Renaissance*. Bloomington: Indiana University Press, 1987.

Johnson, James Weldon, ed. *The Book of American Negro Poetry*. Revised edition. New York: Harcourt Brace Jovanovich, 1983.

Jordan, Casper LeRoy, compiler. *A Bibliographical Guide to African-American Women Writers*. Westport, Conn: Greenwood, 1993.

May, Herbert G., and Bruce M. Metzger, eds. *The Oxford Annotated Bible with the Apocrypha*. Revised standard edition. New York: Oxford University Press, 1965.

Michigan Freedmen's Progress Commission. *Michigan Manual of Freedmen's Progress*. Compiled by Francis H. Warren. Detroit: 1915.

Roses, Lorraine Elena, and Ruth Elizabeth Randolph. *Harlem Renaissance and Beyond: Literary Biographies of 100 Black Women Writers, 1900–1945*. Boston: G. K. Hall, 1990.

Rush, Theresa Gunnels, Carol Fairbanks Myers, and Esther Spring Arata. *Black American Writers Past and Present: A Biographical and Bibliographical Dictionary*. Metuchen, N.J.: Scarecrow, 1975.

Sherman, Joan R. *African-American Poetry of the Nineteenth Century*. Urbana: University of Chicago Press, 1992.

———, ed. *Collected Black Women's Poetry*, 4 volumes. *The Schomburg Library of Nineteenth-Century Black Women Writers*. Henry Louis Gates, Jr., general ed. New York: Oxford University Press, 1988–   .

———. *Invisible Poets: Afro-Americans of the Nineteenth Century*. Urbana: University of Illinois Press, 1974. 2d ed., 1989.

Shockley, Ann Allen. *Afro-American Women Writers, 1746–1933: An Anthology and Critical Guide*. New York: Penguin (Meridian), 1988.

Stetson, Erlene, ed. *Black Sister: Poetry by Black American Women, 1746–1980*. Bloomington: Indiana University Press, 1981.

Washington, Mary Helen, ed. *Black-Eyed Susans: Classic Stories by and about Black Women*. Garden City, N.Y.: Anchor Books, 1975.

White, Newman Ivey, and Walter Clinton Jackson. *An Anthology of Verse by American Negroes*. Durham, N.C.: 1924.

Who's Who in Colored America: A Biographical Dictionary of Notable Living Persons of Negro Descent in the United States. Vols. 1928–29; 1930–32; 1933–37; 1938–40; 1941–44. New York: Christian E. Burckel.

A GARLAND OF POEMS

CLARA ANN THOMPSON

A GARLAND OF POEMS

BY

CLARA ANN THOMPSON

Author of "Songs from the Wayside,"
"What Mean this Bleating of the Sheep,"
"There Came Wise Men," etc.

The Christopher Publishing House
Boston, U. S. A.

DEDICATION

Dedicated to my Brother
Garland Yancey Thompson
In Recognition of his unfailing Kindness
and Affection

TABLE OF CONTENTS

FOREWORD

I have always loved poetry, still my wish has been, to be not a poet, but a novelist. But it seems that the Muse had other plans for me and I have always found myself giving expression to my thoughts in verse. Thoughts that I have intended to express in long chapters of prose, I have expressed in just a few verses of poetry; and I sometimes tell my friends that the writing of poetry has been thrust upon me—I write it because I must—and in presenting this little volume to the public, I do it, not so much with the wish for popularity or fame, but with the satisfaction that I have obeyed the command of my somewhat despotic Muse.

I have endeavored to be sincere and fair in all the subjects treated, especially in those pertaining to my people, whom I love very dearly. So in this book and also in my first book, "Songs from the Wayside," I have endeavored to present both sides of the subject, knowing that no problem can be truly solved in any other way.

A Garland of Poems

UNCLE RUBE ON CHURCH QUARRELS

Brethren, I'm jes' plum' disgusted
  How de churches' takin' on;
'Clare I's nevah seen mo' fussin'
  'Mong de churches since I's bawn.

All a-squabblin' an' a-fightin',
  Some 'bout dis an' some 'bout dat,
Ev'ry whaur you go to meetin',
  'Pears you run into a spat.

Baptist, Methodist an' Christian,
  Most nigh ev'ry church you name,
Done put on de Injun war paint,
  An' I say, it makes me shame;

Makes me shame to see ou' churches
  Stoopin' down to sich disgrace;
Jes' a laughin' stock fah sinners,
  An' a scandal to de race.

Done forgot all 'bout their mission
  Done forgot 'bout savin' souls,
An' a-settin' good examples,
  An' a-teachin' self control.

Yes! done laid aside de Bible
  An' gone pell-mell to de fray,
Usin' all de tricks uv sinners
  Makin' things come out their way.

Jes' won't give no year to reason,
  Heads as hawd as any rock,
Drivin' 'way de earnest seekers,
  An' a-starvin' uv de flock.

I say: Shame upon de churchos,
  Lettin' Satan have sich sw ιy,
When you know dat you kin whop him,
  Ef you fight de propah way.

Fust, we's bound to come together,
  'Case one man can't do it all,
An' ef we don't have no union,
  Tell you what—we's go'n' to fall.

An' we must be mo' in earnest
  See dat ou' own hawts is true,
Puttin' down ou' spite an' envy,
  Trustin' God to help us through.

Ef you's got a triflin' preacher,
  Who's a-travelin' Satan's rout,
An' has jined himself to sinners,
  Rise an' turn de roscal out.

Don't be 'fraid to come agin him,
  Callin' him God's chosen man;
Don't you know ef God had called him,
  He would give him grace to stan'?

Ef He helps de earnest layman,
  To walk worthy in His cause,
Do you think He'd fail de preacher
  Who's a-try'n' to keep His laws?

Even ef de Lo'd has called him,
  An' he falls into a sin,
Handle him; ef he is worthy,
  He'll survive de discipline.

Dat's de way God taught de prophets,
 All dem old time holy men,
Dat ef dey would bear His message,
 Dey must keep their ga'ments clean.

We must drop ou' foolish notions,
 'Case we's all got common sense,
An' de Lo'd ain't go'n'to 'scuse us,
 On de plea uv ignerence.

Fah we promised Him we'd serve Him,
 When from sin He set us free,
So we's bound to fight de debil,
 Make no diff'rence whaur he be.

Den, ef you has got a leader,
 Who's a earnest upright man,
I say, children gather 'round him
 An' hol' up dat preacher's hands.

Fah dah's folks will watch a preacher,
 An' ef he don't show his heels,
Dey ain't got no mo' use fah him,
 Dan 'a wagon wid five wheels'.

Fust to shout when he preach morals
 'Most too high fah human reach,
But dey jes' can't stand him children,
 Ef he practice what he preach.

Now ef you can't drop sich membahs,
 Keep dem undah good control,
(Seems dem ol' wolves in sheep's clothin'
 Will git into every fold.)

An' woe to de church my children,
 Ef dey git de upper hand,
Fah God's troops does sorry marchin',
 When dey's led by Satan's band.

'Taint de hollerin' an' de shoutin',
  Dat's a-makin' uv de saint,
Nor de prayin' an' de groanin',
  No my bredren, 'deed it ain't!

'Tis de life dat you's a-livin',
  Not de shout, de prayer, de groan—
Fah de Bible says, my bredren,
  "By deir fruits dey shall be known."

So it ain't no use to holler,
  'Tain't no use to jump an' shout,
Ef you ain't a-livin' holy,
  Mind! "Your sins will find you out."

An' it is de churches' duty,
  When dese dawk deeds come to light,
To use all de powah God gives dem,
  Tryin' to set de matter right.

Dat's de reason dat ou' churches,
  Often fall below de mawk,
It's because dey're shieldin' membahs,
  When dey know their deeds is dawk.

An' it is dem very membahs,
  Who, when trouble comes along,
Well nigh tear de church to pieces,
  Fightin' always fah de wrong.

Now I know it ain't so easy
  Fah to do de things I say,
But de best we git my children,
  Comes by struggle, not by play.

An' you know dat right is mighty,
  Fah de Lo'd is on dat side;
An' de earnest undertakin',
  He is always dah to guide.

Now I'm go'n' to set down children,
Won't take no mo' uv yo' time,
Fah it seems dah's no end to me,
When I'm talkin' long dis line.

So I'll jes' say in conclusion,
Trust in God, an' press right on!
Fah you'll be here fightin' children,
When ol' Uncle Rube is gone.

YOU'LL HAVE TO COME BACK
TO THE ROAD

You have left the straight highway of duty,
　For the dark winding pathway of sin;
You have cast off the precepts of childhood,
　For the doctrine of world hardened men;
And you wonder why peace has departed,
　Why life seems a wearisome load,
You are lost in the forest of error,
　You'll have to come back to the road.

You have learned to speak lightly of goodness,
　And say that religion's a sham,
You find many faults with the Bible
　And scoff at salvation's great plan;
You say all the world is dishonest—
　Ev'ry man at heart is a rogue;
And you wonder why life is so bitter;
　You have wandered away from the road.

You laugh at the men and the women
　Who have learned to make conscience their
　　guide,
And you say that life is far sweeter
　To those who drift with the tide,
Then you seek in the gay halls of pleasure,
　The peace that has left your abode,
But you'll ever seek vainly, my brother,
　You'll have to come back to the road.

You'll have to come back to the precepts,
　You learned in your childhood's pure day;
Come back to the faith pure and simple,
　Ere the world had lured you away;
Come back to the sweet sacred story
　Of the Friend who bears ev'ry load;
Come back from the far distant country,
　You'll have to come back to the road.

DREAM SHADOWS

Sweet thoughts and vague dreams come to me,
  As o'er the fields the soft winds blow;
The golden sun shines brilliantly,
  The shifting shadows come and go.

And ah, those sweet elusive dreams,
  Come ever drifting from afar,
As golden as the bright sunbeams,
  As shifting as the shadows are.

I try to grasp them—all in vain;
  They linger lightly in my mind,
Then like vague forms, are gone again,
  Leaving a half-sweet pain behind.

Perchance they're ghosts of childish dreams,
  That filled my fancy long ago,
Ere yet I'd drifted down life's stream,
  To where the deeper waters flow.

Perchance they're tones from spiritland,
  So vague so far away, they seem
To me, who cannot understand,
  But echoes of a childish dream.

Ah well, whatever they may be,
  These vague sweet dreams that come and go,
I know they always come to me,
  On days like this, when soft winds blow.

BE SWEET

A happy song sprite is coming my way,
And flooding the air with sweet melody;
He sings in my ears as I pass down the street:
"I bring you a message: Be sweet; be sweet.

"The message is old as the years are long;
And I bring it alike to the weak and the strong,
To the young and the old and to all whom I meet,
What e'er your condition—Be sweet; be sweet.

"The thoughts that are wicked I'd frighten away;
The words that are bitter I never would say,
The tale that is spiteful I would not repeat,
Just heed you my message: Be sweet; be sweet.

"The pathway of life is oft dreary at best,
The sigh often stifles the smile and the jest;
Then cast not your hindrance to clog weary feet,
Be kindly and helpful; be sweet, be sweet."

Still merrily singing, away flew the sprite,
And soon the bright vision was lost to my sight;
But his song still remains, and I ever repeat,
When life would grow bitter: Be sweet; be sweet.

BECAUSE WE KNOW

No matter how the cold winds blow,
    How deep the snow drifts in the vales,
Down in our hearts we know, we know
    Spring breezes follow wintry gales.

We know the flowers will come again,
    And with their sweetness fill the air;
We know we'll look across the plain,
    And see the verdure everywhere.

And so we face the winter's storm,
    Its piercing winds, its sleet and snow,
With hearts where hope is burning warm,
    Because we know; because we know.

And thus it is when woes befall;
    When to our lives the dark days come;
We know that God is over all,
    That brightness ever follows gloom.

We know as sure as spring will come
    To prove we did not hope in vain,
So sure a happy day, will dawn,
    When joy shall triumph over pain.

So oft along the darksome way,
    We walk with faces all aglow;
The star of hope shines steadily,
    Because we know; because we know.

THE PRINCE OF PEACE

(Xmas, 1916)

The Prince of Peace! oh name most sweet and
    holy!
  Dear name through which a dying world may
    live,
That sheds like blessings on the high and lowly,
  The only name that endless life can give.

The Prince of Peace! oh theme of wondrous story,
  Tale, that no mortal e'er can understand—
The Son of God, disrobed of all His glory,
  Descends to earth, to die for sinful man.

The Prince of Peace! oh name so fitly given,
  By men of old unto the Holy Child,
Who willingly forsook the joys of heaven,
  That God and mankind might be reconciled.

Oh Prince of Peace, though war may rend the
    nation,
  And cast its dreadful blight o'er all the land,
In thy own time, oh God of all creation,
  Thou wilt subdue the creatures of thy hand.

Ah, they may rise in pride of power and station,
  And strive to set at naught thy holy will,
But thou art king of ev'ry warring nation;
  They must bow down when thou sayest:
    "Peace; be still."

And so today in praise we lift our voices,
  Oh Prince of Peace, for love that ne'er shall
    cease;
While ev'ry soul that in thy love rejoices,
  Sends up its prayer for universal peace.

"SHOWIN' OFF"

Showin' off! dat's one fault children,
    Dat's a-harmin' of de race;
An' wuss thing—you's like to find it
    Lurkin' in mos' any place.
Find it 'mongst de older people,
    And de youngsters dat you meet,
You kin see it in de churches,
    In de homes, an' on de street.

'Tain't no use to try to stop it,
    Seems it's bound to have its way,
Spoutin' round amongst ou' people,
    An' its got a mighty sway.
Dah! it's gone into de pulpit;
    See dat preacher?—Preachin' fine!
Ev'rybody's eye is on him,
    An' he shows a well trained mind.

But dat scamp is at his elbow,
    Whisp'ring folly in his ear,
An' dat man begins to holler,
    Like he thinks de folks can't hear;
Commence racin' 'bout dat platform,
    Like he don't know whut he's 'bout—
Done got puffed up wid attention—
    Go'n' to make some sistah shout.

An' dem sistahs rise respondin',
    Makin' sich a great to do,
'Case dey're bound to show dat preacher
    Dat dey's got de spirit too.
Can't say I don't b'lieve in shoutin',
    'Case I b'long to dat Ol' School
An' you know dat mos' ol' timers
    Will stick up fah ol' time rules.

But I mus' be straight about it,
  Speak de truth since I commence,
So, ef we will keep on shoutin',
  I say: Let us shout wid sense!
I don't blame de younger people
  Sometimes, when I see dem scoff,
'Case mos' all uv dis great shoutin's
  Nothin' else but showin' off.

Showin' off! Great patience! Children,
  Once I saw two cullud men,
Git to quar'lin' 'bout some trifle,
  Half in fun when dey begin,
Till dey saw de folks wus watchin',
  Den deir wrath rose like a gale!
Nex' dey took one to de dead house,
  An' de othah one to jail.

I come down de street a walkin',
  Feelin' mighty good an' spry,
See two well-dressed men a-talkin',
  One looks up an' ketch my eye;
Den his voice is raised in laughtah,
  Augerment, or mighty scoff,
An' thinks I: Lawd help dat dawky,
  He's done gone to showin' off.

Showin' off has made good women,
  Fill deir homes wid costly things
Pictures, furniture an' cawpets,
  Well nigh fine enough fur kings.
Den go straight into dat washtub,
  Whaur dey labor night an' day,
Till dey's nigh worn to a shadah,
  Gittin' money 'nough to pay.

'Tain't no use in talkin' children,
  I could go on fah a hou'
Till you'd git tired hear'n' me tellin'

'Bout fool things I's seen fo' now—
Dawkies standin' 'bout de sidewalks,
Showin' off to passersby,
Till dey spile a good location;
Makin' 'gainst both you an' I.

'Case you know de unfair white folks—
Put us all into one boat:
"Won't have dawkies livin' 'round us!"
Yes, jes' set us all afloat.
Well, I won't go any furder,
Fah you all know whut I mean,
An' mos' all dese things I'm tellin',
Ev'ry one uv you have seen.

Well, sometimes it sets me laughin',
Den, it almost makes me cry:
People lookin' o'er deir shoulders,
Tryin' to ketch deir neighbor's eye,
'Stid uv lookin' whaur dey's goin';
Nex' dey's fell into de trough,
Children, do git down to bis'ness;
Quit dat tomfool showin' off!

TO OBEY IS BETTER THAN SACRIFICE

Behold, to obey is better than sacrifice, and to hearken
than the fat of rams. 1 Samuel 15:22.

"To obey is better than sacrifice:"
  Rang clearly in his ears,
And knew he not when he turned away,
  That in the after years,
With heart and soul grown sick of strife,
  He would recall this day,
And learn the meaning of the words:
  'Tis better to obey.

But he chose his way, and heeded not
  His Master's clear command;
To him, obedience seemed tame,
  And sacrifice so grand.
He filled his life with mighty deeds,
  And toiled without surcease,
He brought great gifts unto his Lord,
  But sought in vain for peace.
And when death came, with silent tread,
  To bear his life away,
His earnest prayer was: "Lord forgive;
  'Tis better to obey."

"To obey is better than sacrifice;"
  Again the words ring clear,
And a woman heedless passes on,
  Refusing now to hear.
Love's sheltered path is offered her,
  She firmly turns away—
"I'll choose the path of sacrifice,
  'Tis selfish to obey."

"How can I hear the song of joy
    And deem its music sweet,
While all around the suffering ones
    Are sinking at my feet?
Ah no! Their bitter cries of pain
    Would haunt me when I'd pray;
I'll choose the path of sacrifice,
    'Tis selfish to obey."

She chose her path and heeded not
    Another cry of pain,
Because it came from one with strength,
    With power and worldly gain.
But after years had past away,
    She saw that strong man fail,
Saw him his power and strength abuse,
    Saw worldliness prevail,

She looked upon his blighted life,
    And knew he'd failed to stand,
Because he lacked the saving touch,
    Of woman's helping hand.
And knew she then, why, years before,
    The Master bade her stay;
And she too prays: "Dear Lord, forgive,
    'Tis better to obey."

However great the sacrifice,
    The old words still ring true;
'Tis better far to do with might,
    What God would have us do.
To take in faith the lot he gives,
    What e'er false guides may say;
For whether it be joy or pain,
    'Tis better to obey.

BE TRUE TO THE BEST

Be true to the good that is in you,
　The strongest, the cleanest, the best;
Though now it be weak and deficient,
　In time 'twill surmount all the rest.

Be true to the thought that is finest,
　And give the good impulse your heed,
'Tis the noble thought and the impulse
　That warms into life the good deed.

'Tis the patient, sincere cultivation
　Of all that is pure in the heart,
That chokes out the weeds of dissension,
　And bids evil motives depart.

Seek ever the truest, the highest,
　As knights on a Holy Quest;
For your life can ne'er be a failure,
　If you're always true to the best.

PAP'S ADVICE

I ain't got no patience with you;
    Biggest fool I ever saw;
Tell you, I wa'n't no sich coward,
    When I went to court your ma!

Jes' because the gal refused you,
    Fust time that you asked her hand,
You must go 'round here half crazy,
    Brace up boy, an' be a man!

Say your ma is vexed at Jessie,
    Thinks she's try'n' to spile your life?
Did she say how oft I asked her,
    'Fore she said she'd be my wife?

An' ef I had got discouraged,
    Failin' then to do my pawt,
Left her to her woman's notions,
    'Spec' she'd broken both our hawts.

There's a dozen different reasons
    Why a gal will tell you "no",
An', I say, you jes' be thankful,
    'Long as 'tain't another beau.

Sometimes it is only shyness,
    Sometimes pride as like as not,
That sets up a mighty struggle,
    When it finds that she is caught.

Then again she will refuse you,
    'Cause she doesn't know her mind,
While down in her hawt, unknowin',
    She's a-lovin' all the time.

An' ef you be mighty keerful,
  You kin show her where she stands;
It's your place to do the courtin',
  Brace up boy, an' be a man!

An' whatever be the reason,
  Mind you what I say tonight:
Don't you leave the field of battle,
  Till you're sure you've lost the fight.

For a good an' noble woman,
  One that makes a faithful wife,
Is well wuth a man's best efforts,
  You will find in after life.

Your ol' pap knows all about it,
  For he's been all 'long there son,
An' sometimes the hawdest fightin'
  Comes jes' 'fore the battle's won.

OCTOBER

Beautiful, beautiful, golden mid autumn,
  Infinitely sweet, and infinitely sad,
Tinged with a pathos that no soul can fathom,
  Making us grave, and making us glad.

Flooding the earth with a rare, golden sunshine,
  Filling the air with a mystical haze,
Stealing the odor from fruit tree and grape vine,
  Wafting it out to sweeten the days.

Dyeing the trees with the hues of the rainbow,
  Lading the barns with a bounteous store,
While the south winds sweep o'er the green
      meadows,
  Merrily driving the bright leaves before.

Gladly we welcome thy mystical presence,
  After the burden of summer's fierce heat;
Gladly inhale we thy health-giving essence,
  Lending new vigor to tired lagging feet.

Though in the sunlight there's lurking a shadow,
  While in our joy there's a note that is sad,
Yet, willing captives, thy footsteps we follow,
  Making us grave and making us glad.

Beautiful, mystical, golden mid autumn,
    Whence comes the spell thou hast cast o'er the
      earth?
Whence comes thy power, oh magical season,
    Blending so perfectly, sadness and mirth?

LIFE AND DEATH

Written in memory of Dr. Booker T. Washington, the
noted colored educator and lecturer.

We live, and how intense is life!
So full of stress, so full of strife,
So full of hopes, so full of fears,
Of joy and sorrow, smiles and tears;
And oh how fruitless is the quest,
Unless we're striving for the best.

We die; and oh how sad is death!
How sad, when we relinquish breath,
When all life's glory slips away,
And leaves us but a mass of clay.
How sad, and oh how dark the night,
Unless we've found eternal light!

This, of our brother we can say—
We meet to honor him today,
Because he fought life's battle well;
He stood where heaviest missiles fell.
Oft wounded in the crucial test,
Still, ever striving for the best.

Still striving, he has fallen now,
We've placed the laurel on his brow,
While in our hearts, we wonder why
God called this man so soon to die.

We wonder; oh, how blind are we!
His rugged path we could not see;
We only saw his wealth and fame,
His noble station, honored name.
We need not envy him his place,
Who seeks to lift a trodden race.

God knew how hard and well he'd fought,
The noble deeds his hands had wrought;
God heard the deep sighs of his breast,
He heard—and gave the warroir rest.
And shall we weep and say 'tis night,
When he has found eternal light?

IN ANGEL'S GUISE

Darkness abounds; what seemed at first
    to be the voice of God,
Has proven but an empty sound
    by wayward fancy made;
I walk alone; and though deep gloom
    enshrouds my path,
    I'm not afraid.

For this I know: though voices false
    may whisper in my ear,
As on I go, and seek to lure my steps away
    to paths unknown,
God will not let my feet go far astray,
    He'll keep His own.

I feel no fear; although His presence
    now I can not feel,
I know He's near, to guard and guide,
    to give the strength I ask,
And when the devil comes in angel's guise,
    To lift his mask.

THE FLIRT

No indeedy! I'm not caring,
  Let them hang around and pine,
If I didn't break their fool hearts,
  They would be a-breaking mine.

Men are mighty funny creatures,
  Keep things on the highest shelves,
Then they'll break their necks to get them,
  Jumpin' fit to kill themselves.

Keep things down where they can reach them,
  And just see them pass them by!
Still a-lookin' and a-jumpin'
  For the things they know's too high.

No indeedy! I ain't caring!
  Though they pine an' fume an' fret,
And just break their necks a-trying
  None of them have won me yet.

HE HAS ALWAYS CARED FOR ME

No, my Lord has never failed me,
　And how can I doubt him now?
Though the winds howl fiercely 'round me,
　And the spray is on my brow,
Though the billows wildly raging,
　Lash my ship far out to sea,
Naught I fear, and naught can harm me,
　He has always cared for me.

Oft before, on life's wide ocean,
　Storms have tossed my ship at will,
But always, in His good season,
　He has spoken: "Peace; be still";
And I do not fear to trust Him,
　Though full dark the way may be,
For I know, deep in my bosom,
　He has always cared for me.

No, my Lord has never failed me;
　In life's darkest, saddest hour
He has made me feel His presence,
　Feel His all-sustaining power,
And when joy has been my portion,
　He has made mine eyes to see,
His kind hand in all my gladness,
　He has always cared for me.

Then, can I with this assurance
　Go in fear along life's way,
Mindless that a Friend so faithful,
　Guards my path from day to day?
No! my doubting sinks before it,
　And my heart cries joyfully:
"Blessed Lord! I'll ever trust Him,
　He has always cared for me."

THE NEW SCHOOLHOUSE

Mt. Healthy, Ohio

"We want a new schoolhouse" the wise neighbors
    said;
  "A school on a modern plan;
A school that that our townsmen can point to with
    pride,
  As one of the best in the land;
For the great hand of Progress is seen ev'rywhere;
And our dear old town must have her full share.

"Besides, they are crowded, the teachers all say;
  The old building here is too small,
New scholars are coming in day after day,
  We'll have to accommodate all."
So they talked and they planned and wise was
    their scheme,
But the new school house was still but a dream.

The architect came with his papers and plans,
  And he laid before them his sheet,
That showed how the school should be inside and
    out,
  And how it would look when complete.
When he'd finished, the building could almost be
    seen,
And yet the new schoolhouse was still but a dream.

And then came the workmen with muscular arms,
  With strong and capable hands,
Who turned into substance the wise neighbors'
    dream,
  And the architects well ordered plans.
So today we behold, with faces abeam,
This beautiful building—this realized dream.

And as we assemble, with speeches and song,
  To dedicate this, our new school,
We would say to the pupils: Be faithful; be
    strong;
  Let honor and diligence rule.
And dream your bright dreams, for bright dreams
    are your due;
But remember 'tis work that makes them come
    true.

CONQUEST

The battle was fierce; he was worn and spent,
  And beaten down in the fight,
But he faintly said, as he sank to the earth,
  "I'll die with my face to the light."

"The goal that I sought, I never shall reach,
  I feel the approach of night,
But I'll die with my face towards the setting sun,
  I'll die with my face to the light."

Bewildered he gazed on the golden crown,
  That in heaven greeted his sight,
But the Father said: "He is conqueror
  Who dies with his face to the light."

HE HAS BIDDEN ME GO FORWARD

He has bidden me go forward,
  In a path I've never trod,
And I'm not afraid to venture,
  Not afraid to trust my God.

For in all my years of service
  He has been so true a guide,
That I dare tread any pathway,
  When I know He's at my side.

And since He bids me go forward,
  Though I cannot see the way,
Yet I will not doubt nor falter,
  But will trustingly obey.

For through darkness or through sunlight,
  Through the cold or through the heat,
If o'er shadowed by His presence,
  To obey His will is sweet.

HE COMES NO MORE

I am thinking tonight, as the old year dies,
  Of one who has passed to the other shore;
And my heart is sad when I realize,
  How true are the words: "They return no
    more."

For crowding each other, the years rush by,
  And we gather to watch them breathe their last;
But he never comes with his smiling eye,
  To watch with us, as he did in the past.

And he never comes when we meet to sing
  The songs that he loved so well to hear;
Nor e'en when the troubles and cares press in,
  To lighten our hearts with his words of cheer.

And he never comes—But why should I start
  The blood from that half-healed wound again?
For it's God alone who can soothe the heart,
  When its beating time to that sad refrain.

Oh, list! the bells are beginning to ring,
  And my heart is filled with a vague unrest;
But I know whatever the year may bring,
  Will come from the One who knows what is
    best.

INGRATES

They come to us with bleeding hearts,
  And eyes by tears made wet;
We bind their wounds, we dry their tears,
  They leave us,—and forget.

When grim ill-fortune comes their way,
  We find them at our door.
We welcome them with outstretched hand,
  And share with them our store.

And when our time of trial comes,
  Our day of stress or pain,
It finds us knocking at their door,
  We knock,—but knock in vain.

TEMPTATION

She read the story of a love most deep,
  A love wherein all thoughts of self were lost;
A love that sowed and asked not: "Shall I reap?"
  A love that never paused to count the cost.
And thoughtfully she laid the book aside,
The face of him who sought her for his bride
Came to her heart, and bitterly she cried:

If this is love, I feel no love for him
  Then what is this that bids me make this choice?
I seem to hear amid the shadows dim
  The calm insistent whisper of a voice
That bids me listen to his earnest plea,
But now a darksome doubt is haunting me,
If this is love, I know it can not be.

Is it because I know that he is good,
  That people say his heart is pure as gold,
I've let my fancy wander as it would,
  And lightly grasp the prize I may not hold?
And still the voice says: "Listen to his plea"
But oh I fear 'tis pride and vanity,
That bids me venture where I cannot see.

And love for love has been the age long cry
  Of hearts that struggle through the maze of life,
And naught but love, pure love, can satisfy,
  Can win the race, or triumph in the strife.
Then shall I listen to his earnest plea,
And give him naught but pride and vanity,
When he would give his best, his all to me?

And yet, ah me! that voice will not be still;
   That voice that bids me listen to his plea;
Worn with the strife, I let it have its will,
   And only pray, harm may not come to me.
The voice within is ever urging me,
His voice without is pleading constantly,
I fain would yield and ask not what it be.

Ah, as I'm yielding light breaks o'er my way,
   I gladly rouse me from my troubled dream,
And see with eyes made clear by heaven's day,
   The surging dashing falls just down the stream.
And thankfully I steer my boat ashore,
I know beyond a doubt, the strife is o'er;
I hear the Voice—the Tempter's voice no more.

OUR SOLDIERS

*Written on the occasion of the colored troops
leaving Cincinnati for Camp Sherman, to train
for the World War.*

Today the din of Europe's strife,
 Is sounding at our very door;
No longer heard, with bated breath,
 As echoes from a foreign shore.
No more the distant war alarms,
For at our door, they call to arms.

They call to arms—and our own boys
 Must answer that grim call today;
Oh, how our fond hearts follow them,
 As gallantly they march away
With steady tread and fearless eye,
To bravely do or bravely die.

We've prayed for others, kinsmen dear,
 And others, friends who've marched away,
But there's a new note in the prayer,
 That rises to the throne today.
And Europe's battle fields seem near,
Since those we love must soon be there.

Yet, fear we not for our brave boys,
 Our colored troops that march away,
For ne'er yet has a swarthy son,
 Disgraced the flag they bear today.
Forgetting wrongs when foes come in,
They never fail the call for men!

OUR HEROES

Written on the occasion of the return of the colored troops to Cincinnati, Ohio from the World War.

We crowded on the pavements,
　To see our boys march by;
Our soldier boys, with faces grave,
　But vict'ry in their eyes.

They left a few short months ago,
　For Europe's battle din;
They left us, jolly laughing boys,
　They came back grave faced men.

For theirs it was, to blaze the way,
　On that dread field of blood;
They shrank not from the giant task,
　But fearlessly they stood,

And held their ground like iron men,
　And fought as demons fight,
Their foes were fiends for tyranny,
　But they were fiends for right!

Ah no! those black boys knew no fear;
　Knew no such word as "yield";
The German troops in terror, fled
　Before their deadly steel.

They blazed the way to victory;
　We cheer till out of breath,
To see them marching, stalwart men
　Back from that field of death.

Yes, back again with laurels won;
  Our hearts are beating high;
We knew they'd fight as heroes fight,
  And die as heroes die.

We knew that when they fought in France,
  They'd gain an honored place,
For there they judge men by their deeds,
  Regardless of their race.

The whole world knows the story now,
  Then, will their homeland dare,
To still withhold the liberty,
  They fought so well to share?

Now let us pause, with faces bowed,
  While reverent silence reigns;
In mem'ry of those valiant boys,
  Who came not back again.

AUTUMN-TIME

'Tis Autumn-time, 'tis autumn,
  I know it by the trees,
I know it by the mystic haze,
  That hangs above the leas.

I know it by the moaning winds,
  And by the sobbing rain,
And all the multitude of signs,
  That follow in her train.

The farmers, bringing in the corn;
  The frost-nipped flower and vine;
The children laden down with nuts;
  All speak of autumn-time.

And oh, some days are golden,
  And some are gray and sad,
So like our lives is autumn-time,
  Mingled with grave and glad.

COMMUNION PRAYER

I feel oh, so unworthy, Lord,
    To drink thy cup today,
But when thy dear voice bids me come,
    I dare not stay away.

I've tried so hard to do thy will,
    So hard to worthy be,
But oh, dear Lord I fail so oft,
    When I would honor thee.

I know not why thou bidst me come,
    Unless dear Lord it be
That thou wouldst prove thy mercy great,
    And tender love to me.

So I receive with grateful heart,
    Oh blessed Savior mine,
In memory of thy sacrifice,
    This sacred bread and wine.

THE COMMON LOAD

Aw'ed by the sight of earth's o'erwhelming woe,
   The ceaseless cry of suff'ring human kind,
I said: "Be still"; unto my troubled soul,
   "Their weight of grief is greater far than thine.

"Thou art but weary with the common load;
   The burden that all human hearts must bear;
Why press thou selfishly unto the Lord,
   To pour into His ear thy petty care?"

I ceased my plaint, and plodded on my way,
   But longer ever longer grew the road,
Until at last, worn out, I knew not why,
   I sank half-fainting 'neath a nameless load.

And lying there, too weak to think or pray,
   The scene in far Judea came to me,
When weary mothers brought their little ones
   And pressed them babbling, to the Master's
      knee.

And His disciples bade them stand aside:
   "Why vex the Master wtih thy cares so small,"
But Jesus, knowing said: "Forbid them not."
   And blessed the little children one and all.

The vision vanished, but I understood;
   And gladly leaned I on the gentle breast
Of Him who says to ev'ry weary one:
   "Come unto me, and I will give thee rest."

GOIN' TO FOOT IT ALL THE WAY

(Aunt Betty Testifies)

Brothers an' sisters, I've been trav'lin'
  Many years on heaben's road;
I ain't lookin' for no char'ot,
  Ain't a-frettin' 'bout my load,
I ain't mindin' my ol' ga'ments
  'Cause the dust has made them gray,
'Took my cross upon my shoulder,
  Goin' to foot it all the way.

I don't 'spect to find all roses
  While I'm trav'lin' on this road,
'Cause I know that ev'ry Christian's
  Got to bear some sort of load;
Got to walk some paths of sorrow,—
  Got to watch and fight and pray,
I done took my cross up brothers,
  Goin' to foot it all the way.

Jesus didn't have no char'ot
  When He went to Calvary,
With His cross upon His shoulder,
  There to die for you and me.
Tho' the burden was so heavy,
  That He sank upon the way,
An' good Simon had to help Him—
  Goin' to foot it all the way!

Yes indeed! I'm goin' to foot it;
  Be the journey short or long;
When I'm weak I'll be a prayin',
  An' a-singin' when I'm strong;
An' the Lo'd will bid me welcome,
  When I reach eternal day,
Bless God! On my way to glory!
  Goin' to foot it all the way!

EASTER, 1919

Easter with skies transcendently bright,
  Easter with hyacinths blooming;
Easter with message of hope and light,
  Gladly we welcome thy coming.

War and disease have swept o'er the land,
  Leaving it wounded and bleeding;
Come, for the world disconsolate stands,
  Come with thy balm for its healing.

Millions see naught besides the white cross,
  Where a brave soldier lies sleeping;
Millions bewail grim pestilence's cost,
  Come thou, and silence their weeping.

Tell the sad hearts that Christ conquered death,
  Give them the message from heaven,
Incense more sweet than hyacinth's breath—
  Christ has thrown open the prison.

Come to the tomb in the garden today,
  Where the great stone is now rolled away,
Then hear the angel triumphantly say:
  "He is not here: he is risen."

A REPROOF

You had no cause to speak that unkind word,
  What matter if her faults to you were plain?
You saw her staggering 'neath her heavy load;
  Why add your wormwood to her bitter pain?

You know her heart is always kind and true,
  Whate'er her foibles or her faults may be;
You know when care or trouble comes to you,
  She's ever ready with her sympathy.

And all must need plead guilty to some fault,
  Then why in face of grim Misfortune's frown,
Make it a sword to stab a fellow-man?
  'Tis never brave to strike when one is down.

OUR DECEASED LEADER

Written in memory of Herbert Moninger, A. M.
B. D. well known leader in Sunday School work,
Cin., Ohio, and read at memorial service.

We thought his work only half finished,
  But God said: "His work is all done;"
And swinging ajar heaven's portals,
  Said: "Enter thou brave faithful one.

"Thou hast finished the work that I gave thee—
  To shed a new light on my Word—
Well done thou good faithful servant,
  Enter thou the joy of thy Lord!"

But we stood like sheep without shepherd,
  Like men when their brave leader falls,
In the midst of a fierce raging battle,
  When he answered his Master's call.

And our hearts rose up in rebellion—
  Why had the Lord called him to go,
While still his great work seemed unfinished
  While still the world needed him so?

Then came, like a soft benediction,
  The mem'ry of what he had taught,
And it soothed our hearts into silence,
  With the healing balm that it brought.

He taught us God's goodness and wisdom;
  He taught us to bow to His will;
And though he is no longer with us,
  We follow his teaching still.

And now that our God in His wisdom
  Has taken our dear leader home,
We bow, though not understanding,
  And whisper: "Thy will be done."

"I HAVE LIVED FOR THIS HOUR"

Written in memory of Mrs. Mattie Sikes.

All worn out with sickness, and dying, she lay;
They watched with sad faces, her life ebb away;
"Is it well?" some one asked as she sank 'neath
    Death's pow'r,
"Oh yes", came the answer, "I have lived for this
    hour."

"Long, long years ago I chose Him my guide,
Have striven through life to keep close to His side;
And now at the end, He is still my High Tower;
I've nothing to fear; I have lived for this hour."

Ah blest life of service! she made Christ her king,
And then she lay dying, but Death had no sting,
A bright crown of splendor, and heaven her dower
Oh, 'tis well worth a lifetime to live for that hour!

OUR IDOLS

We set up idols in our hearts,
  That hide our God from view,
And worship them so fervently,
  Not knowing what we do.

We bring to them for sacrifice,
  Our dearest hopes, our all—
Then wake to find them wood or stone;
  God help us, when they fall!

THERE CAME WISE MEN

The world pressed hard; his faith was dim,
And he could not hear the Christmas hymn,
The angels sang o'er hills afar,
Where wond'ring awestruck shepherds were.

He could not go with the joyful men,
To the manger-crib in Bethlehem,
The world pressed hard; he'd lost the way,
And he could not find where the Christ-child lay.

The Christmas shoppers filled the street,
While happy children, close at his feet,
Gazed long, with eyes all wonder wide,
Through windows decked for Christmastide;

Their faces bright with a faith as deep,
As the men of old who watched the sheep;
And he sighed and said, as he went his way:
"The angels' song is for such as they."

"For such as they; not busy men
Who must meet the world's dire stress and sin,
Who need must battle with giant might,
Or be trampled down in the bitter fight."

And he sighed again as he pressed his way
Through shoppers, chatting merrily,
With parcels every shape and size,
And the Christmas gladness in their eyes.

Then he glimpsed in the throng, a face so drear,
That it seemed to blight the Christmas cheer;
And all day long, persistent, grim,
That gloomy sad face haunted him.

Till there came to his heart, an impulse strong,
To make the sad ones hear the song.
"What matter if no song I hear?
I can bring to others the Christmas cheer."

And he followed where e'er that impulse led,
Through the crush and din he pressed ahead:
Where e'er there were deeds of love to do,
That impulse led—unerring, true.

And he unquestioning, followed on;
Then found at last, that his doubts were gone,
And the impulse strong that had led him afar,
Transformed into a radiant star.

He followed the star through the crush and din,
And lo! it led to Bethlehem;
To Bethlehem! Oh wondrous ray!
To the manger crib, where the Christ-child lay.

And he found as he knelt to worship there,
Where the angel chant late filled the air,
That shepherds knelt, but not alone,
There were Wise Men too at the manger throne.

THE MINOR KEY

"Oh for a song" the poet sighs,
"To stir men's hearts and make them rise
    To heights of nobleness!
A song whose clarion notes will ring,
Long after I have ceased to sing,
    And heal life's bitterness.
Alas! this is the fate for me:
To ever sing in a minor key."

A thousand hearts echo the sigh,
    Brave hearts that struggle on alone,
With aspirations pure and high,
    With deeds forgotten or unknown.

They hear the proud world laud the great,
    They watch the cheering crowds go by,
And bitterly lament their fate—
    Oh foolish hearts, subdue that cry!

What matter if the world forgets,
    Thy deeds to laud, thy tale to tell?
    If God remembers, all is well;
With Him who sees not as we see,
No life is tuned to minor key.

THE CHRISTMAS CHOIRS

'Tis Christmas morn; and o'er the earth
   The sound of music rings;
For Christ is born, and joyfully
   The choir of angels sings.
To Bethlehem the shepherds come,
   To find the infant king;
To Bethlehem the wise men come
   Their praise and gifts to bring;
And back to heaven sweeps the choir,
   That came His birth to sing.

'Tis Christmas morn; and o'er the earth
   The sound of music rings;
For human hearts have caught the song,
   And joyfully they sing.
The simple ones and wise ones come,
   To worship Christ the king,
And e'en the little ones have come
   Their infant praise to bring;
And over all, the human choir
   Its joyful anthems sing.

AUNT MANDY'S GRANDCHILDREN

"Look here children! who's this coming?
  Why it's old Aunt Mandy Payne,
With her basket and her bundle
  And that big old-fashioned cane.

"Come right in! Give me your basket;
  How've you been, you sweet old dear?"
"Oh I've had a sight uv trouble
  Chile, since last time I wus here."

"You don't say! (Give me that bundle)
  (Now you children run and play)
And what were you saying Auntie?"
  "Why Nell's Jane has run away."

"You don't say so! What a pity!
  Nell was careless with that girl;
Let her run down there to Turner's;
  Wouldn't have done it for the world."

"Well, Jane was Nell's only gal child,
  An' she couldn't say her "no";
But it wusn't 'cause Nell spilte her
  Dat made dat chile take on so.

"Run away wid dat low dawky,
  An' she's not yet turned sixteen;
Married to dat triflin' rascal—
  'Who'd she marry?' Turner's 'Gene!

"Yes done run away an' married,
  An' sich talk you never heard;
Turned to sassin' me an' Nellie,
  No! we couldn't say a word.

"Said 'she guessed she knew her bizness,
　Mother Turner wus her friend,
She had been more sympathetic
　Than we two had ever been.

"Umph! that jes' set Nellie crazy!
　An' it made me mighty sick,
But I seed as quick as lightnin'
　Somepin' else—the chile wus tricked!

"Yes indeed! dat's what's de matter,
　An' I jes' tol' Nellie so;
Fust she tried to talk me out'it,
　But at last she let me go.

"An' I want to tell you honey"
　(Here Aunt Mandy's voice grew low)
Dah's a spell on all Nell's children
　Dat is whut I'd have you know!

"Fust 'twas Jim; he took to stealin';
　Den Bob took runnin' roun'
Wid dem triflin' low-life dawkies
　Dat you find in ev'ry town.

"Now it's Jennie—Nellie's baby,
　An' I spec' 'twill break her hawt;
Oh a spell is on dem children,
　Kinder b'lieved it frum de stawt.

"An' I jes' 'bout know who done it;
　I'm a-watching ev'ry sign;
An' I'll tell you all about it,
　When I've satisfied my mind."

Then, Aunt Mandy, nodding wisely,
　Went 'to see de chaps a while,'
And the younger woman watched her,
　With a thoughtful, half-sad smile.

"Poor old fashioned, love blind granny!
Any one outside could see
How they humored all those children
What the consequence would be.

"So she thinks it's conjuration;
Hard to change when one is old;
Well, if that will help her bear it,
Let her b'lieve it, dear old soul!"

SPRING'S PROMISE

The Spring returns, and all the land is beaming;
 The birds come back from Southland's sunny
  clime;
The earth with signs of waking life is teeming,
 All move in harmony to nature's time.

The grass is springing up in yonder meadow,
 The trees are putting forth their tender leaves;
Across my window flits a tiny shadow—
 The birds are nesting 'neath the cottage eaves.

Where e'er I turn there's hope and joy and glad-
  ness,
 And life, new life, sweet springtime's agelong
  sign,
And yet, for some there rings a note of sadness—
 Spring comes with life, but leaves their dead
  behind.

Ah, well may come glad Easter at this season,
 When waking life on hill and field and plain,
Wrings from sad hearts the cry of blind unreason
 For those they know can never come again.

But Easter comes, proclaiming: "He is risen!"
 "Come see the place where once thy Lord didst
  lay;
And know ye this: that when He broke His prison,
 The stone from ev'ry tomb was rolled away!"

Oh blessed hope unto all sad hearts given!
 And waking life on hill and field and plain,
Rings sweet with promise sent to us from heaven,
 Look up! Rejoice! thy dead shall live again.

THE SETTLEMENT WORKER'S PRAYER

I pray for those about me here,
  I strive to make them good and true,
And then my heart cries: "God help me"
  For oh my Lord, I need thee too.

They bring their tales of woe to me;
  They ask me Lord, what they shall do;
I bring them with their woes to thee,
  And oh I bring my burdens too.

Dear Lord, I would not selfish be,
  But thou knowest well my strength is small,
And oh thou knowest too dear Lord,
  That should I falter, they might fall.

And so I earnest pray to thee,
  That thou wouldst make them good and true;
And when thy blessing comes to them,
  Oh, loving Savior, bless me too.

CONSECRATION

Oh God, whose wisdom, well I know
  Can still this world's unrest,
Set up thy kingdom in my heart;
  I dare not pray for less.

How can I bid men call on thee,
  To still their troubled souls
While aught but thy almighty pow'r
  Within my heart controls?

I fain would tell men how thy pow'r
  Has kept my hot heart still,
And thou canst do the same for them,
  I know thou canst and will.

No strength of mine, nor intellect,
  Have saved me from the fall,
So trusting in thy pow'r alone,
  I consecrate my all.

Rule thou supreme within my heart,
  Oh, God of righteousness!
That I may bring thy healing balm,
  To others in distress.

LET US GET BACK TO GOD

Oh, men and women, high and low,
　　Who ev'ry path have trod,
And know not whither now to go,
　　Let us get back to God!

The world is full of dark unrest,
　　Of woe and strife and sin,
Of hearts, hard, bitter and distressed,
　　Worn out with problems grim.

And women wailing drearily,
　　And men with fury red,
Their hands o'erfilled with luxury,
　　And yet they cry for bread.

They see not blessings when they come;
　　They're blinded by unrest;
Their lips to gratitude are dumb,
　　They know not happiness.

Dark Envy with his blighting train
　　Is sweeping through the land,
And peace and happiness lay slain
　　Beneath his blasting hand.

Men covet talent, wealth and fame,
　　And join in envy's strife,
Neglecting gifts God gave to them,
　　To make a useful life.

They scorn the simple laws he gave,
　　To make the least sublime,
And so o'er earth there sweeps a wave
　　Of restlessness, and crime.

No pow'r on earth can stay this tide,
　Or lift us from the clod,
No pow'r on earth nor ocean wide,
　Let us get back to God!

The God who e'er did sovereign hold,
　Though earthly monarchs fell;
The God of Abraham of old,
　The God of Israel.

The mighty God who ever leads
　His hosts to victory,
And heals their wounds, supplies their needs,
　Unless they disobey.

But ever since the world began,
　When nations hold their sway,
Regardless of Jehovah's plan,
　He turns his face away.

He turns His face away and then—
　Behold Confusion's reign!
Of war and pestilence and sin,
　Unrest, and greed for gain.

And nowhere find they happiness,
　But 'neath His staff and rod,
With all our problems and unrest,
　Let us get back to God!

FAINT HEART

You say you love the lady fair,
    Your heart is full of woe;
I wonder if, oh craven heart,
    You've ever told her so!

You blame her for her haughty pride,
    And say she ought to know;
I blame you for your cowardice
    If you've not told her so.

And even if she's heard your sighs,
    And thinks your love is true,
If you have never said a word,
    What can the lady do?

Despite the many theories
    And all the notions new,
The modest maid still waits, until
    Her lover comes to woo.

So if you ask me for advice,
    I say with ne'er a doubt,
That if your love is worth the name,
    You'll write or speak it out.

THE MOTHERS DEAR

The mothers dear: God bless them!
The mothers young and fair;
The mothers dear: God bless them!
With silver in their hair.

The mothers dear: God bless them!
The mothers old and young,
Throughout all generations
Their praises will be sung.

The men of ev'ry station,
Wealth, poverty and fame,
When asked to judge the mother,
Their verdict is the same.

We hear from highest places
Familiar words, but true:
"I owe to my dear mother
The worthy deeds I do."

We hear another saying:
Who trod the whirlwind's track,
"My mother's love and counsel
Found me and brought me back."

And to their testimonies,
We gladly add our own:
That our own faithful mother
Was sweetest ever known.

And while with grateful homage
The mothers' praise we sing,
Let's breathe a prayer for that one
Who has no wedding ring.

MORE THAN NINETY YEARS

On the ninety-first anniversary of Union Baptist Church, Cincinnati, Ohio.

If they could be with us today,
  As we review the work we've done,
I wonder, friends, what they would say,
  Those veterans of '31.

They wrought when hope was burning low
  For men of color in this land;
Before God struck with mighty blow,
  And slavery fell beneath his hand.

And still they wrought with courage strong,
  This little band of freemen true,
And proved they, to the doubting throng,
  What this down-trodden race could do.

They dared to do what colored men
  Of weaker courage dared not do—
They strove to be intelligent,
  And still unto their God be true.

God understood for what they strove
  And stooped to cherish and protect:
For one of Satan's strongest foes,
  Is God-directed intellect.

So this church struggled on and grew,
  Her battle e'er for God and right;
With aim still high and ideals true,
  She stands today, a beacon light!

Yes all these years this church has stood;
  Those early warriors are gone;
Yet all these years, the fight for good,
  Has e'er been bravely carried on.

The years will pass, and still she'll stand;
  Though she has faults, yet she will win;
For ev'ry church, as ev'ry man,
  Must battle with besetting sin.

'Tis trusting God that cleaves the way;
  She's trusted more than ninety years;
Were those old founders here today,
  They would be smiling through their tears.

RAYMOND G. DANDRIDGE

Cincinnati's Invalid Poet

An angel came to scatter gifts
 Among earth's restless throng,
And to this noble invalid,
 He gave the gift of song.

So lying helpless, on his couch,
 He sings from day to day,
Despite discouragement and pain
 That press him constantly.

Too brave to beat with helpless wings
 Against his prison bars—
God gave those helpless wings the strength
 To soar among the stars.

For with his book of verse in hand,
 We read it page by page,
And think: Birds sing their sweetest songs
 Oft times within a cage.

He fights his battle with a strength,
 We scarce can understand;
Despite his helplessness and pain,
 He's every inch a man.

I DREAM

I dream, I dream;
I dream because it's sweet to dream;
I know the dream will ne'er come true,
Another's voice is calling you,
And you will answer "yes" some day,
And follow him where e'er he may.
    And yet, I dream.

I dream, I dream;
I dream because hope is not dead;
It still lives on; I know not why;
For well I know some day 'twill die,
And I shall feel a stab of pain,
And know I can not dream again;
    Till then, I dream.

BUT HERE BY HIS SIDE IT IS CALM

We press close, close to the Master,
　And "Lead us Lord" we pray;
For out in the world the storm beats hard,
　And many are losing their way.

Out there is the boom of the thunder,
　And the clouds are sweeping low;
The cries of the lost and the wounded,
　As, staggering on, they go.

Out there with no guide for their footsteps,
　For their bleeding hearts no balm,
Out there the storm rages fiercely,
　But here by His side it is calm.

Out there where the fierce storm is raging,
　Men sell their souls for gain;
And women forget they are women,
　In the strife for things that are vain.

Out there are soldiers who follow
　But ever afar from their Guide;
They know not the blessed communion,
　Of those who keep close to his side.

'Tis there that we learn how His presence,
　Can brighten the darkness of night,
Why he tells us his yoke is easy,
　The burden He gives us is light.

CHILDHOOD AND MAY

Far, far adown the aisles of time,
  The sprites are dancing merrily.
Their faces beam, their bright eyes shine,
  But lo! tis but a memory.
A memory of childhood days,
When earth was full of sprites and fays.

They blightely walked the woodland ways;
  Or scampered through the waving grass,
And peeping out, with cunning gaze,
  Would watch the happy children pass.
So very near, yet out of sight;
Ah, cunning were those childhood sprites.

And bears were wise in those fair days,
  They were not always rough and wild,
Oft times they'd take a child to raise,
  And how we longed to be that child!
Ah happy thought! ambition rare,
To be reared by good Mother Bear.

And oh, the springtime of that day!
  The season to our hearts most dear.
And springtime's crown—the first of May,
  The sweetest day in all the year.
May Day, with skies forever fair,
And scent of blossoms everywhere.

And how the birds sang in the trees!
  Such songs ne'er now from bird throats rise;
Such humming insects, buzzing bees,
  Such gorgeous flowers and butterflies!
No wonder fairies, sprites and fays,
Roamed o'er the earth on those May Days.

We did not dance in childish glee,
　　Around the May pole on that day,
But happy as the birds were we,
　　And celebrated our own way.
May Day we cast our shoes aside,
And barefoot, trod the meadows wide.

Such races, such athletic feats!
　　Then, that our feet from weights were free,
Our field day program was complete,
　　And light of foot as deer were we.
While those who did not love such play,
Roamed through the woods the livelong day.

Ah, far adown the aisles of time,
　　The sprites are dancing merrily.
Their faces beam, their bright eyes shine,
　　They're keepers of our memory!
Our memory of childhood time,
When earth was full of mirth and rhyme.

A CALL TO SERVICE

He bids me rise; he bids me go
To grapple with the mighty foe;
He bids me speak; he bids me stand,
I dare not counter his command,
    For He's my God, my king.

I go, though round my path the darts
Fall thick and fast—may pierce my heart;
I dare not falter in the fight,
He bids me stand— the God of Might,
And He's my Lord, my king.

I go, though see I not the way,
I go; my task is to obey;
The mighty God who gave me breath,
'Tis His to give me life or death,
    Mine to obey my King.

A voice above the roaring sea
Says naught of harm shall come to me,
And though sometimes my courage fails,
I know 'tis but the flesh that quails,
    My soul says: "All is well."

And so with all my strength I go,
To grapple with the mighty foe;
The foe that fain would crush my race;
I meet him boldly face to face;
I fear not his ferocity
For God is mightier than he,
    And in his strength I'll win.

BEREAVEMENT

The Angel of Death claims our loved ones;
He claims them again and again;
But we never get used to the partings,
And we never get used to the pain;
So our hearts are heavy—so heavy
And our tears are falling like rain.

So dear to our hearts are our loved ones,
And each holds a place all his own;
A place that belongs to no other
We ever shall know, or have known,
And a place forever is vacant
When one from the circle has flown.

No wonder we weep when death calls them,
E'en though we know they're at rest;
No wonder the Father bends closer
That we may lean on his breast;
For the hardest of all of life's lessons
Is: learning His way is the best.

WHAT MEAN THIS BLEATING OF
THE SHEEP?

And Samuel said, What meaneth then this
bleating of the sheep in mine ears, and the lowing
of the oxen which I hear? 1 Samuel 15:14.

America, proud freedom's land,
　Thy flag is trailing in the dust!
Where are thy boasted precepts grand,
　Thy pledge of faith: "In God We Trust?"

Thou criest to the world's oppressed,
　Who stretch to thee appealing hands,
"Come hither, come! here end thy quest,
　Thou'lt find a refuge in this land."

"This land of love and liberty,
　Far-famed in history and song;
Where Justice holds supremacy,
　Where God is feared and faith is strong."

Oh, cease thy boasting freedom's land!
　'Twere sweeter far to hear thee weep;
If thou hast heeded God's command,
　What mean this bleating of the sheep?

Thy founders fled, with hearts aflame
　With freedom's fire, across the waves;
Ere long, to them the Tempter came,
　And offered them a band of slaves.

Alas! they failed, those founders proud,
　And as they gained in freedom's power,
There followed ever, like a cloud,
　The shadow of that testing hour.

And when they stood, from England free,
A voice came from that shadow deep,
E'en while they shouted "Victory",
"What mean this bleating of the sheep?"

For lo! they rose at Freedom's call,
And rent their galling chains away,
But left the black man still a thrall,
Without a hope of Freedom's day.

And so that warning shadow spread,
Until it covered all the land;
And civil war, the nation's dread,
Clutched at its throat with bloody hands.

And brother strove with brother then,
Upon that awful field of blood,
Until the fettered African,
Before the world, a free man stood.

Alas! they did not loose his bands
Because they hated slavery,
But that their fair united land,
Might ever undivided be.

And so they broke the galling chains,
And bade the African go free;
But cast a stigma on his name,
That blighted all his liberty.

In this great Freedom's land he saw
That other nations refuge found,
While prejudice's cruel law
In chains of thralldom held him bound.

He saw the laws that make men free,
For him grow feeble from disuse;
And boasted Christian charity
Sink to oppression and abuse.

Again we hear the solemn words,
  Forerunner of King Saul's defeat—
"What mean this lowing of the herds,
  What mean this bleating of the sheep?"

For more than fifty years have passed,
  Since you declared the black man free,
And still your fetters hold him fast,
  Bound in that other slavery.

You care not that he's proved his worth,
  You care not for his loyalty;
The land that gave the black man birth
  Has proved his deadly enemy.

You block his pathway to success,
  By force, deceit, and strategy;
And oft your brutal prejudice,
  Finds outlet in the mob's wild sway.

You cause for mobs you'd glorify:
  The black man's crime 'gainst womanhood.
And while you flaunt the baleful lie,
  You hound the women of his blood.

Yes, hound them till you bring them low,
  Protected by your laws unjust;
Then call them vile names, when you know
  They're but the victims of your lust.

How dare you boast of chivalry,
  And haste to shed the black man's blood,
While you, like wolves, feast greedily
  On unprotected womanhood?

You, lifting guilty hands to God,
  Vow universal liberty;
While 'neath your feet, the trampled sod
  Reeks with the blood of tyranny.

Your brother's blood, though dark his face,
  Shed by the fiendish mob's decree;
His crime? A member of that race
  You've held long years in slavery.

You dragged him, bleeding, through the streets,
  To where you'd built a ghastly pyre;
You tortured him like savage beasts,
  Then cast him, living, in the fire.

Your mothers with their babes were there,
  To view that feast of fire and blood;
Your sisters, wives and sweethearts fair,
  God pity such base womanhood!

Oh proud, vain women of the South,
  You also have a work to do!
For jealous pride has sealed your mouths
  Till you've become the victims too.

Too proud to own your sister's wrongs,
  Or say your men do aught amiss,
You languish in your broken homes,
  Or join in revels such as this.

Yes, revels that should make you blush;
  Instead, you lend a helping hand
To make your lauded Sunny South
  The fest'ring plague spot of the land.

Arise! Arise! count not the cost!
  Where is your boasted Southern fire?
That nation is forever lost
  Whose women sink into the mire.

America, proud freedom's land,
  Your flag is trailing in the dust!
Where are your boasted precepts grand,
  Your pledge of faith: "In God We Trust?"

Did you thus trust Almighty God,
  The blacks would have their liberty;
Nor would you wait until His rod
  Drives you again to set them free.

How dare you say you trust your God,
  And keep your mob and Ku Klux Klan?
Did you thus trust Almighty God,
  You'd scourge the monsters from the land!

Had you such faith, your Freedom's vow,
  You made to God, you'd dare to keep;
And He would not be asking now:
  "What mean this bleating of the sheep?"

He asked that question years ago,
  And well you know the price you paid;
Your streaming blood, your cries of woe,
  A bitter lamentation made.

He speaks again; you'll not obey;
  You raise weak arms against his might,
But soon there'll come a bitter day
  When he will scourge you to the right.

E'en now your wards from foreign lands,
  Are forging chains of Anarchy;
And while you chain the African,
  They'll bind you in their slavery.

You welcome knaves to liberty,
  But scorn the loyal African;
You'll learn the worth of loyalty,
  When Anarchy invades the land.

Beware, America, the proud!
  Thou'lt surely bitter harvest reap;
Once more there comes in accents loud:
  "What mean this bleating of the sheep?"

Seek not like King Saul by device
    An answer to that question deep;
Who said it was for sacrifice,
    He spared the cattle and the sheep.

For God beheld his sinful heart,
    And spoke the words of doom to Saul;
Unless thou from this sin depart,
    America, thou too, shalt fall!

OUR SIDE OF THE RACE PROBLEM

I come to you, my countrymen,
   Come with and earnest plea,
I pray the God of Israel,
   That you'll lend ear to me.

For, like those murm'ring men of old,
   You wander in distress;
You've left Egyptian slavery,
   To find the wilderness.

You've left the land of Pharaoh,
   And deem that you are free,
But lo! a hundred foes arise,
   To claim your liberty.

I speak not of the barriers,
   Your proud white brothers place,
I'm speaking of the deadly foes,
   That rise in your own race.

Division, lust and slavishness,
   Envy and jealousy,
Your disrespect for your own race,
   And lack of charity.

The proud white man betrays your trust,
   Your faith he never blunts,
Him you forgive a hundred times,
   Your poor black brother—once.

You gladly see the white man rise
   To wealth or to renown,
But when a black man fain would rise,
   Your envy drags him down.

You care not for the pain you give,
  Your motto seems to be:
"No colored man upon this earth
  Shall be ahead of me."

How can we rise if none excel?
  Where will our leaders be?
Our envy and our selfishness
  Destroy our unity.

We cannot be the christian race
  That we profess to be,
And lack the greatest grace of all,
  The grace of charity.

'Tis easier to close our eyes
  And soar in heavenly flight,
Than plod along life's rugged way
  And treat each other right.

But though we soar in rhapsody,
  And view the realms above,
We'll fail—and we shall always fail,
  Until we learn to love.

You say more faith and joy and hope
  Than any race have we;
The Bible says that these are naught,
  Devoid of charity.

That charity that envieth not,
  That's patient, true and kind;
Sweet charity! the only grace
  Our scattered race can bind.

Oh be not like the Pharisees,
  Who other faiths abhorred,
And placed their faith above all men's—
  Then crucified their Lord.

You say that slav'ry's blasting curse
  Still has you in its toils;
E'en though it be, yours is the task
  To loose the serpent's coils.

Despite the white man's prejudice,
  Despite his treachery,
You still will cast your race aside,
  To give him loyalty.

The white man comes with lustful love,
  A deadly serpent's slime,
You deem it honor and romance,
  When it but leads to crime.

You give the children of such love
  A high and honored place;
You scorn the black man's baseborn child,
  And shrink from that disgrace.

While white men's blood at any cost,
  You count among your gains,
They hate your blood, and brand the man
  With one drop in his veins.

Oh friends of mine, how can you rise
  To power and liberty,
With such distorted slavish views
  Of pride and chastity.

How can you rise? how can you rise
  With such a weight as this?
You sanction by your self-disdain
  The white man's prejudice.

You would the white man's equal be,
  With strength his onslaughts meet,
Then 'stead of standing at his side,
  You grovel at his feet.

What gain you by your servile mein,
    Your meek and lowly place?
For when you kneel to shun his blows
    He kicks you in the face.

Arise! Arise! stand on your feet,
    For take this truth from me:
No nation e'er has yet been known
    To crawl to liberty.

The law may give us equal rights,
    The boon our nation craves,
But if we stand not on our feet,
    We're still the white man's slaves.

God made all nations of one blood,
    And we his servants be,
Then dare we cast his word aside,
    And bow to man's decree?

You call it by a gentler name,
    And hope to 'scape the rod—
Wrong will be wrong and sin be sin,
    As long as God is God.

Whenever God gives a command
    He gives strength to obey,
'Tis only when our faith is weak,
    We fail to find the way.

Then rise, ye men of pure black blood,
    And mixed blood—brothers all,
Away with slavish vanities,
    Arise at manhood's call!

Your people, in the foeman's toils,
    Cry out for liberty,
Yours is the task, to rise like men,
    And help them to be free.

Cast envy and intrigue aside;
 Join in the nobler strife—
Help your divided race to rise
 Into the broader life.

Yours is the task their rights to gain,
 Their safety to secure,
And fight as other men have fought,
 To keep your women pure.

Your women! oh 'tis God alone,
 Knows what they've had to bear,
Of slavery's curse, and aftermath
 They've had a double share.

Your arms by slav'ry paralyzed,
 Have proved a feeble stay,
In consequence, too oft, too oft
 They've been the white man's prey.

But when you learn to stand like men,
 To cherish and protect,
To sympathize instead of blame,
 You'll win their deep respect.

'Tis only by the power of God,
 That they have bravely stood,
And kept their courage and their faith,
 Their strength and womanhood.

Your women! oh you need not fear,
 That they will not be true,
For when you bravely lead the way,
 They'll gladly follow you.

And now be patient, friends of mine,
 I have just one more plea,
God bids me speak, and oh my friends
 I dare not silent be.

My plea to ministers of God:
  You too must take your stand,
And teach your people what it means
  To be a godly man.

If God has called you from the world,
  His ministers to be,
Then walk before the world like men
  Of strength and purity.

'Tis true that Satan often hurls
  His sharpest darts your way,
But if you truly trust in God,
  You need not be his prey.

God holds his children safe within
  The hollow of his hand;
Then if he's called you to his work,
  He'll give you grace to stand.

For shepherds cannot lead their flocks
  The straight and narrow way,
While they themselves are wandering,
  And going far astray.

Men wonder why so oft you fail,
  When comes the crucial hour—
You sacrifice sincerity,
  And godliness for power.

Led on by pride, you often make,
  A lordship of your call,
When Christ has said: that he who leads
  Must servant be of all.

Know you what meant he when he said:
  Leaders must servants be?
He meant: They serve their fellowmen,
  With Christ's humility.

Humility that makes all tasks
However great or small,
A noble service for our God,
Who's king and Lord of all.

And oh you ministers give heed,
Or God, who understands,
Will give the task He's given you,
Into more faithful hands.

Lead on your flocks, oh men of God,
And this your watchword be:
All glory to the King of kings,
Who gives us victory.

Teach them to truly worship God,
Not idle dreamers be;
Help them to learn the law of love,
And live consistently.

Lead on! and may God give you strength
And courage to endure;
For if a fallen race would rise,
Her prophets must be pure.

THE BONDS OF SERVICE

We strain at the chains that bind us,
    And struggle to be free;
We'd leave our burdens behind us,
    And fly to liberty.

We'd cast off the things that fret us,
    The trials hard to bear,
The many cares that beset us,
    The duties ever near.

Yet, somewhere I've heard so truly,
    The echo still remains,
That he who would live life nobly,
    Is bound by a hundred claims.

And only those who are selfish
    Can boast full liberty,
How noble the bonds of service!
    Why struggle to be free?

SHE PRAYED

One morning in the long ago,
   I stole in from my play,
But paused beside the open door
   To hear my mother pray.

My mother who had lain so long,
   Upon a bed of pain,
And knew full well that health and strength,
   Would ne'er be hers again.

She prayed; I stood in childish awe
   And listened to her prayer;
She prayed as only mothers pray,
   She knew not I was there.

She prayed for her three little girls,
   Such tiny maids were we;
I wondered vaguely at her fears,
   Too young the path to see.

She prayed; awestruck, I listened there;
   She told God all her fears,
As I stole back to play again,
   That prayer was in my ears.

The memory of many things,
   Slipped from my childish brain,
But oh, the mem'ry of that prayer,
   Forever shall remain.

One little maiden stole away,
   Ere two short years had gone,
And joined the mother whom she loved·
   The others journeyed on.

And when I see how safe they've come,
   Through all the changing years,
I whisper with a grateful heart:
   "God heard my mother's prayers."

SOMETIME, SOMEWHERE

Sometime, somewhere in ev'ry life,
　There comes the need of God;
We may not recognize the truth,
Or cast it off in pride of youth
Or manhood's sophistry,
But there can be no substitute
　When comes that need of God.

Along life's beach what wrecks are strewn,
And ships have gone to ports unknown
　Tossed by storms that prevail,
When man bows not his stubborn will,
Nor lets the Master say "Be still,"
　To winds that toss and flail.

Sometime, somewhere, in ev'ry life
　There comes the need of God;
Where e'er you be, whoe'er you are,
Your ship will have a broken spar,
Your life will bear imperfect fruit,
If seek you for a substitute,
　When comes that need of God.

CIRCUMSTANTIAL EVIDENCE

Scot dashed into his sick wife's room;
  "What's happened Dick?" she said.
Breathless, he flung a heavy sack
  Beneath his sick wife's bed.

He scarce had time to turn around,
  For in two minutes more,
The farmers close upon his heels,
  Were knocking at his door.

"Dick Scot, we've come to search your house!
  'Bout caught you in the trick;
Come now, you needn't say a word,
  We're goin' to do it Dick!"

"Well, search de house den, ef you will,
  An' git thu wid it quick,
But don't you dah to search dat room
  Wha' my po' wife lays sick."

"Scot, you had chickens in that sack,
  You know as well as I,
You bought your groceries yesterday,
  We ain't goin' let you by.

"We count on searching ev'ry room,
  For Jones here saw you run;
I'll bet you've hid the chickens there"—
  Scot sprang and seized his gun.

Then standing in the sick room door,
  With blazing eyes, said Scot:
"De fust man steps across dis sill,
  I shoots him on de spot!

"I know you's got no 'spects fah me,
  I know you, ev'ry one;
Ef I cain't check you wid my words,
  I'll check you wid my gun.

"Ol' Dick Scot knows a thing er two;
  You whitefolks ain't de law;
You come hyar try'n to play wid *me*,
  You'll find de lion's paw.

"Yes search de house! Yes search de house!
  Who keers fur ol' black Dick?
But don't you dah to come in hyar,
  Wha' my po' wife lays sick."

The farmers searched the other rooms
  And, grumbling, went away;
Scot packed his things that very night,
  And moved to town next day.

He knew the alley where he'd go
  The farmers never went,
So on the air, as he drove off,
  A ringing laugh he sent.

"Shame on you Dick;" his sick wife said;
"Well honey, whut's de use,
Nigh all we git fum dese white folks
  Is scoffin' an' abuse."

No neighbors near, none saw him go;
  And when three days had gone
They came—and found the house and yard,
  With feathers overstrewn.

"EXCEEDING RICHES"

AND OTHER VERSE

by

J. PAULINE SMITH

Compiler of "Olive Prints"
(A Year-Book of Quotations from Robert
Browning's Poems)

Detroit, Michigan

1922

A. M. E. BOOK CONCERN
PHILADELPHIA, PA.

Affectionately Dedicated to
MOTHER
Whose lullaby songs were all from the Methodist Church Hymnal

PREFACE

Acknowledgement of the following magazines, religious and secular papers, in which some of the verses herein originally appeared, is hereby made: "Detroit Young Women" (the former publication of the Young Women's Christian Association of Detroit), "Detroit Club Woman," Detroit Leader, Detroit Free Press and the Christian Recorder, Philadelphia. Under the title "The Heart of Christmas," a gift booklet was printed in 1917, containing the verse for "Festival Days." These with others, hitherto unpublished, have been included in this little volume and sent forth in the hope that they may be of interest to a wider circle of readers.

THE AUTHOR.

November, 1921.

(v)

A FOREWORD

The crying need of the world to-day was
adequately stated in the Summer (1919) num-
ber of "Le Livre Contemporain." "The war,"
says this writer, "showed the utter futility of
materialism—of the age of science, and if
civilization is not to fail again, we must cen-
ter our lives and ambitions not on things ma-
terial, but rather on things of the spirit."

The verses found in this slender volume are
an expression of this life of the spirit. Their
author, like Wordsworth, or even more like
Milton, triumphs over every vicissitude of
fortune because her mind is fixed upon the
eternal, hence nothing temporal can perma-
nently depress her spirit or destroy her abid-
ing joy and peace. Such writers, whether un
known or well- known, have a message for
mankind; and those who pause and read these
lines will have their minds and hearts refresh-
ed and strengthened, and their spiritual eyes
uplifted to the Lord, from whence cometh our
help.

THERESA SMITH, B. Pd.

(vii)

[103]

CONTENTS

FESTIVAL DAYS

MISCELLANEOUS

MEDITATIONS

"EXCEEDING RICHES"

(Eph. ii: 7-8)

O grace Divine, it saves me now!
  With riches free doth me endow;
I once was blind, but now I see
  Redemption plann'd so wondrously!

O grace Divine, it saves me now!
  And sets God's favor on my brow;
It plants my feet where angels tread,
  With life eternal crowns my head!

O grace Divine, it saves me now!
  My Saviour's mercy I avow,
But shall not know till face to face
  "The exceeding riches of His grace!"

THE UNIVERSAL LANGUAGE

'Tis not spoken by the tongue of man
    Nor uttered by his voice;
It needeth not interpreter
    To make the heart rejoice.

We hear it in each glad new day
    That comes to me and you;
In starry gleams at night it speaks
    From heaven's o'er-arching blue.

Its sweeter sounds are treble tones,
    The thunder is its base;
If 'tis a voice most powerful,
    'Tis also full of grace.

'Tis gone abroad thro' all the earth,
    Where'er men see and hear,
Nature's myriad voices tell
    The Mighty God is near.

MADE ONE BY THE GLORY

You have seen at sunset how the crimson and
    the gold
Unite in wondrous radiance that doth all things
    enfold:
The lowly cottter's dwelling and stately walls
    of stone,
In lavish'st adornment is this golden splendor
    thrown.
'Tis the miracle of eventide when day's dis-
    cordant story

Is harmonized to beauty by the sun's depart-
ing glory.

No one knows the glory that was our Saviour's
own
Before He left the light and life about the
Father's throne,
But is it not the greatest thing in His high-
priestly prayer
That He should in that happy state permit us
all to share?
That here, perhaps at eventide, all creeds' con-
fusing story
Shall merged be in one by the greatness of
His glory!

HOW MUCH MORE?
(Heb. 9:14)
Forthwith every need supply,

If a loving earthly parent
　Heareth when his children cry,
If he always gladly seeketh
Shall not God, our Heavenly Father,
　Who is rich in boundless store,
Good things give to him that asketh,
　Give in bounty, how much more?

If, again, that earthly parent
　Would not substitute a stone
For the bread that nature craveth,
　When the cry comes from his own,
Shall not God, our Heavenly Father,

On our thirsty spirits pour
All the quick'ning of His Spirit,
　　Fullest measure, how much more?

If the blood of bulls and fatlings,
　　Freely on the altar given,
Brought to mankind—erring, sinful,
　　Gift of cleansing down from Heaven,
Shall not then the blood of Jesus
　　Wash us, purge us and restore
Our dead consciences to service,
　　By its power, how much more?

How much more!　O, how much more!
　　Than the richest parent's store,
Shall not God, our Heavenly Father,
　　On us His Holy Spirit pour?
Shall not Christ, our blessed Saviour,
　　More than offerings of yore,
Purge us, cleanse us, "How much more?"

────

LOVE'S WORK

Oh, the life that loves is the life that lives,
　　That lives and never dies.
To the soul that loves the Saviour gives
　　A home beyond the skies.

Oh, the heart that loves is the heart that grows
　　That grows more like to Him;
To the heart that loves the Saviour shows
　　Himself, the light within.

For love alone makes life worth while,
And love is from above;
It clothes us with the Saviour's smile,
For God Himself is love.

———

"CALL ME ISHI"

(Hosea 2:16)

"Call me Ishi," Church of God,
I for thee the wine-press trod,
All my glory did forego
To woo thee from the Prince of woe,
"Call me Ishi."

"Call me Ishi," lonely one;
I will be thy shield and sun;
I'll thine every need supply;
When in danger, I'll be nigh;
"Call me Ishi."

"Call me Ishi," nevermore
Other lovers to adore;
Thee, I in righteousness betroth,
Mine alone from now henceforth,
"Call me Ishi."

A PRAYER FOR THE TIMES—1914

Oh, in these days of war's array,
We would unceasing daily pray,
Where gay externals nigh had won us
Lord, let Thy beauty be upon us;

Above all grace of form or skin,
Lord, make us beautiful within;
Like Moses, may our faces shine
With that rare glory caught from Thine.

In lieu of robes of costly price,
Lord, may Thine estimate suffice:
And we esteem it passing fair
The Spirit's lowly garb to wear.

THE "GREATER ONE"

(Luke 11:31)

Exerywhere you reverent turn,
Can you not in truth discern
Here the presence-room of One
Greater than King Solomon?

In the blue of yon clear sky,
On the grass where pearls lie,
In the pure, ambient air,
Speaks there not Jehovah's care?

In the peace that reigns at dawn
On a glorious summer morn,
Breathes there not assurance clear
That the Prince of Peace is here?

In the matin-song of bird,
This sweet undertone is heard;
"It is I, Be of good cheer!
Lo, the 'Greater One is here!' "

"MORE THAN OTHERS"

(Matt. 5:47)

The "more than others" people,
  Don't you love them though!
In business, church and social life,
  How they keep the world aglow!

Going always one mile farther
  Than a friend requests:
Working ever somewhat harder,
  While some tired one rests.

Loving where no love is given,
  When there's no reward:
Saluting not alone their brethren
  Following their Lord.

These "more than others" people,
What a vital place they fill!
And their ranks are never crowded,
  Won't you join their guild?

A DEDICATION

Holy Spirit, I give myself to Thee,
  Do as Thou wilt with me:
  Chasten, reprove, refine,
  So Christ's life may shine
  Through me to men,
And souls be born again!

Holy Spirit, I give myself to Thee,
  That Thou my Guide mayst be
  In all the paths of Truth,
  So that aspiring youth
  May Christ's own image see,
Reflected clear in me!

Spirit of prayer and praise,
  Grant in these latter days,
  When wolves attack the fold
  And love oft waxeth cold,
  That I, baptized anew,
May stand steadfast and true!

"GOOD THINGS TO COME"

(Heb. 9:11)

Such things as prophets in the days of old
Did so much long Jehovah would unfold;
Just how the daily sacrifice should cease,
And leave no need of temple veil and priest;
How One, a lamb before his shearers dumb,
Should be for man of offerings the sum,
The fruitage of their hopes—"Good things to
    come."

Such things as in the fullness of the time
Did come to pass, making the Earth sublime;
So that the chosen Twelve could all rejoicing
    say:
Our eyes have seen the life, the Truth, the
    Way;
Within the temple courts no need of traffic's
    hum,
Henceforth its rites and ritual are dumb
Before the Word made flesh: "the good things
    to come."

Such things the Master must have had in view
When to the Twelve He said: "Much greater
    shall ye do";
Such things as came with Pentecost, and since
    that day
Have blazed for the Church a shining way;

Such things as make all other voices dumb
To those who know their Christ as Priest, the
     sum
Of present joys; and still—"Good things to
     come!"

GOD'S SCALES

How much weigh you to God?
His are unerring scales,
So finely set the balances
Adjustment never fails.

Are you so full of faith,
And deeds of holy love,
That they'll amply weigh for you
With Him who dwells above?

Is yours the moral worth,
And more, the heart so free,
That you can meet His final test:
"Leave all and follow me?"

How much weigh you to God?
For after all our vaunting,
None at last would hear Him say:
"Weighed, and found wanting."

"HE THAT KEEPETH ISRAEL"
(Ps. 121:4)

Sometimes, o'erworn by many cares,
We are too weary for our prayers;
Then, how assuring it is to know,
As we to rest confiding go
That He who doth His Israel keep
Hath not our human need of sleep;

That dear ones, near and far away,
    For whom we may not conscious pray,
Are kept, and we have peace serene,
    Because there watches One between
Who safely guards His scatter'd sheep,
    And doth dot not cease His watch for
        sleep.

And then how oft when dawns the day;
    When we to work betake our way,
Though open-eyed we fail to see
    The snares escap'd by you and me,
Because He who ever guards His sheep
    Doth neither slumber take nor sleep!

"PLEASURES FOREVERMORE"
(Ps. 16:11)

O ye, so burdened here with care,
    No time for pleasure have to spare;
And ye whose purses are too short
    To surplus leave for happy sport,
Who spend, perhaps, what you might save
    To make another's path less grave,
Because your hearts are running o'er

With love for One who sorrows bore,
For you, of pleasures, He hath store
  At His right hand forevermore!

O ye, whose wage no margin yields
  For gladsome strolls in verdant fields;
For leisure hours to idly spend
  On ocean's beach till summer's end;
Or cruise 'mid Nature's lovely scenes—
  Adown her myriad inland streams;
O ye whose scanty little store
  Forbids much wandering from the shore,
Yet, rich in faith, your pleasures soar,
  At His right hand forevermore!

"At His right hand?" It is not far,
  Indeed, 'tis just beyond the bar.
You breathe not long the close land-air,
  Which seems so very hard to bear,
When other barks put out in glee,
  Know all the fresh joys of the sea;
But you shall know as saints of yore,
  To suffer is to taste life's core,
And on those higher pleasures pore,
  At His right hand forevermore!

A LESSON FROM GIDEON

What riches in the Word one finds
  In reading 'twixt the marginal lines!
There, in the wars by Judges told,
  What vistas doth this fact unfold:
The Spirit of God did rest upon
  Or "clothe itself with Gideon!"

Gideon, just the earthly dress
  Through which the Spirit did His best;
Just the mouth and hands and feet
  To make the work of God complete.

Oh, in these days when so much care
  Is given to the clothes we wear,
When we, more than we like to own,
  Think so much of a pretty gown,
How it doth kindle us to read
  This line about the Spirit's need!
That He, to follow God's behest,
  Must take us for His earthly dress!
For this, O Spirit, make us meet
  To be Thy garb, Thy work complete!

SOME PROMISED BLOOMS
(Isa. 61:11)

Though anemone and violet
  Regale the woodland ways,
Some fairer blooms are promised yet:
  E'en righteousness and praise.

Which, as Earth puts forth her bud,
  And causeth things to grow,
He, who sendeth all of good,
  Shall for all nations sow.

Hence, flowers silent heralds are,
  For as they spring and grow,
We know there hasteth, tho' afar,
  His own great floral show.

A CONTRAST

"Nothing is known,"
The Cynic said,
And sadly bowed his learned head.
"We mortals here—a mimic show—
May much surmise, but nothing know.
The Past? evolution disagrees:
The Present? so near, no one rightly sees;
The Future? mere wild hypotheses."

"One I know,"
The Christian said,
And raised aloft his trusting head.
"The One who keeps my sacred trust,
Redeems us from the mocking dust.
"The Past? God the dower;
The Present? kept by His power; .
The Future? Faith's crowning hour."

ASPIRATIONS

O, Christ of Galilee,
Make Thyself known to me!
Thou, who didst the hungry feed,
Let me know something of the need
Of hungry souls:
That none may empty go away
For want of word that I should say.

O, Christ of Bethany,
Make Thyself known to me!
Thou, whom households loved to greet,

Let me learn also at Thy feet
    The love that folds
All human loves within its own
And scatters joy as light is sown.

    O, Christ of Calvary,
        Make Thyself known to me!
Thou who gavest all so willingly,
Let mine be just such love for Thee,
        That naught withholds;
Nor counteth not the human cost
Which spreads the glory of Thy cross.

IS YOUR NAME AHISAMACH?

(Suggested by a lesson in the "Drop-in-Bible Class," Y. W. C. A.)

Of all those queer old Hebrew names,
Which each a special meaning claims,
There is none one would more gladly own
Than that by Bezeleel's helper borne:
Ahisamach, "supporter of a brother,"
Would you not love above all other?

Upon your arm does some one lean?
By some one's side can you be seen,
In some dark, crucial, trying hour,
To save her from the Tempter's power;
Swift to supply a sister's lack,
Is your name Ahisamach?

Have you the love that some one needs?
Some heart that sadly droops and bleeds

For fellowship and some true friend
To whom to go, on whom depend,
For help along life's upward track,
Is your name Ahisamach?

When one is fainting beneath her load,
And tired, too, because of the road,
Is yours the ready word of cheer
To make that load less hard to bear?
Or to lift it from a sister's back,
Is your name Ahisamach?

Oh, life would easier, sweeter be,
For other souls near you and me,
Should we so wholly in Him trust,
His strength so perfect be in us,
He to our names could add this other,
"Ahisamach, supporter of a brother."

"BERECHAH"

(2 Chron. 20)

Forth to meet their enemies,
  Those men of Judah went—
At the word of God by the prophet
  Who to their king was sent—
In the dewy dawn of the morning,
  To the wilderness of Tekoa,
With no arms or ammunition,
  Save to shout God's praises o'er!

They march'd to meet three armies,
  Who had up against them come;
But, fearing not, they trusted God,

Who sent their praise shafts home;
For the "liers-in-wait" were angel bands,
  And more confused were they
Than if the men of Judah had
  With weapons won the day.

Then, after the unfought battle
  And the taking of great spoil,
When their foes all were vanquish'd
  Without their martial toil,
Because the battle was the Lord's,
  And He had fought for them,
They paused on the homeward journey
  For a glad thanksgiving hymn;

Paused in a lowly valley,
  Where, their gratitude expressing
In songs so high and jubilant,
  Made it the vale of "Blessing."
From that blest day and forward,
  For the hearts uplifted there,
They called that joyous trysting-place,
  "Valley of Berechah."

COMMUNION

Just to go apart with Jesus,
Just to hear His still, small voice;
Just to wait upon His message,
Just to know He is my choice:

Just to hear my Saviour speaking
In the stillness of my soul;
Just to have the waves of blessing
O'er my waiting spirit roll;

O, 'tis sweetest of all pleasures
Thus to steal away to Him!
Thus to be alone with Jesus
And to feel His peace within.

I would often seek my Saviour,
I would never leave His side;
I would go forth in His presence,
And would in Him e'er abide!

FULLEST LIFE

If Christ were living full in me,
How radiant my life would be!
How lost ones would Thy glory see,
If my poor heart continually
Kept open house alway for Thee!

Lord, of that living water give,
That I may in Thy fullness live;
O grant that there may daily be,
That well upspringing glad in me,
Refreshing, 'midst life's stress and strife,
Thy well-spring of eternal life!

If Christ were living full in me,
How luminous my life would be!
How it would shine far out to sea
And heaven-ward point unerringly
Had Christ abiding place with me!

If Christ were living full in me,
His risen life so rich and free,
How He would lead to victory.
And life abundant mine would be,
Self crucified and merged in Thee!

"THOUGH OUR OUTWARD MAN PERISH"
(2 Cor. 4:16)

"Though our outward man perish,"
    Worn by work and care,
If the Holy Spirit nourish,
    The inner grows more fair.

"Though our outward man perish,"
    Grows weak to human view,
As the Holy One doth cherish,
    The inner man's made new.

"Though our outward man perish,"
    At the call of mother clay,
The inner man shall flourish
    Unto the perfect day!

"ACCOUNTED WORTHY"
(Luke 21:34-36)

To stand before the Son of man
    Unshrinkingly,
When from His face, in that dread day,

Heaven and earth shall flee away,
To be accounted worthy then to stand,
Upright and calm at His right hand,
Our Lord, alone, makes known the way:
    "Watch and pray!"

To stand before the Son of man
    Preparedly;
Not freighted so with earthly cares,
That day approach us unawares;
But, like those virgins, wise, to be
Ready the bridegroom's face to see,
Our Lord alone makes known the way:
    "Watch and pray!"

To stand before the Son of man
    Victoriously,
When that unnumbered host shall come
For word of welcome, or of doom;
To be deemed worthy palms to wave,
White-robed, among the final brave,
In that fire-testing, judgment-day;
Said He, the Life, the Truth, the Way:
    "Watch and pray!"

"JEHOVAH SHAMMAH"

(Ezek. 48:35)

A vision of the ideal city,
    The exiled prophet saw,
And set it forth in all the beauty
    That dwells in perfect law.

A city where Jehovah's glory,
  Once lost thro' sin and pride,
In this seer's redemption story
  Is seen to ever abide.

A city where a river floweth,
  Which doth such vigor give,
That it is said, where'er it goeth,
  All living things shall live.

A name was to the city given,
  That told what made it fair:
As it for God had humbly striven,
  'Twas called: "The Lord is there."

THE WINNOWING-FAN

When o'er the rich and golden grain
There swept that quaint old winnowing-fan,
So swiftly parted was chaff from wheat,
The threshing-floor became a judgment seat:
Where husks were burned or blown away,
And the grain stored up for a coming day.

Thus John, while pondering it all o'er,
In the wilderness by the Dead Sea's shore,
Saw how this odd, old winnowing-fan
Portrayed the work of the Son of man:
How the clear light of His righteousness
Would be henceforth man's winnowing test

So true this picturesque metaphor,
Once used by John, who went before!
For still wherever Christ has come,
He's brought this sifting process home:
We're blown like chaff to the winds amain,
Or we rest in His garner as golden grain.

A NAME

So well he wrote and with such power,
  Such logic, clear and keen,
Men call the epistles from his pen
  Of very right—"Pauline."

They breathe the spirit of a man
  Who, counting not the price,
So loved and served that he could say,
  "For me to live is Christ."

In after years how it must thrill
  And mould the life, I ween,
When parents o'er baptismal vows
  Have named a child—"Pauline."

"WE AN INCORRUPTIBLE"

What things men do for crowns that fade,
  For laurels lasting but a day!
What willing sacrifice is made
  For just a wreath that will decay!

We, listed in a race where all
  Receive unfading crowns of life,
May count those transient garlands small
  To be but victors in this strife!

THE CALL

The great "I Am" still speaks to men,
Still hears the needy's cry, I ken;
Where they in hopeless chains are bound,
Some one will find it "holy ground,"
And turn from keeping sheep to see
The old Mount Horeb mystery:
Why burns the bush with living flame,
And yet its outline is the same!
In that hour on his ears shall fall
The great, all-thrilling service call:
And, awed and doubtful though he be,
He'll humbly answer, "Lord, send me."

KINSHIP WITH CHRIST

(Matt. 12:50)

Perhaps we may not trace our line
On pages where the records shine
With deeds of worth in town or state,
Which place some men among the great;

Perhaps earth-honored pedigree
Has fallen not to you and me;
But, list ye to the King of kings,
As He a higher kinship brings!

"Whoso," said He in tenderest love,
"Shall do my Father's will, above,
The same is kindred unto me—
Shall mother, brother or sister be!"

Father, we pray, Thy Spirit send,
Grant as our aim, our life's great end;
To kinship have with the King of kings,
And the deathless fame such record brings.

"THEY SHALL SEE HIS FACE"

However cloudy be their days,
However strenuous their ways,
They know, who put their trust in Him,
These things that "wear the thickness thin,"
But bring them nearer to the place
Where "they shall see His face!"

O Face! that just to look upon
Shall mean their highest ideals won!
For when they see that visage fair,
They shall themselves its likeness wear.
Earth's fiercest tests shall leave no trace
When "they shall see His face!"

Oh, how it shoots through all the years
A light that dissipates their tears!
Who love Him know, whate'er betide,
That one day they'll be satisfied:
That day when they, O wondrous grace,
Behold that thorn-crowned, holy Face!

"THIS BEGINNING OF MIRACLES"

"Fill the water-pots with water,"
  They filled them to the brim.
At this word the Master spake
  When Mary turned to Him;
Now draw out and bear, He said,
  Lo. following His behests,
The festal wine is crimson red
  They bear unto those guests!
Then that one whom Jesus loved,
  Divined the wondrous story,
That this beginning sign there
    proved—
  Made manifest His glory.

"THAT I MAY KNOW HIM"
(Phil. 3:10)

To know Him! O aim sublime,
Surpassing all the quests of time;
Pursuit of gold, of wealth or fame
Holds no such charm as Jesus' name!

To know Him! On coming morrows
To better know the Man of Sorrows—
The Christ our heavenly Father sent—
Is purpose high and life well spent.

To "know Him!" the Apostle flings
This word as he enraptured sings:
"All other things I count but dross
To know the glory of the cross!"

"NEITHER"

Neither rites, nor creeds, nor churchly forms
    Avail with God above;
One thing alone His word requires:
    Faith which works by love.

Neither Jew, nor Greek, nor bond, nor free;
    No man by birth is known;
From Scythian shores or isles of Greece,
    They all in Christ are one.

No one is high, no one is low,—
    There is no great nor small;
All human lines sink out of view
    And Christ is all in all!

"THREE THINGS"

(On hearing a sermon to children from Gen. 26:25)

Three things within the narrative
  Are writ of one of old,
Whose name meant Laughter, and whose
  Life held symbols manifold;

Wherever on his journeyings
  This pilgrim chose to dwell,
He altar built, pitched his tent,
  And then he digged a well.

An altar and a tenting-place
  Should our life's story tell;
Then thirsty ones who follow us
  Will find a living well.

GOD'S "BEST," NOT OURS

God cannot fully use the man
  Whose aim is just "the best" he can;
To fill our souls with holy fire,
  More than our "best" does He require.

It burned upon the lips of Paul.
  Who more abundant wrought than all;
With His strength as my guarantee,
  All things can be performed by me.

Thus, the searching service test
  Is not our boastful human "best;"
But through us and how mightily
  Has worked the Christ of Galilee.

REMEMBERED LANDS

O land, remembered after years
  Of waste and devastation,
O land, sought out by God again,
  Thy people made a nation!

O exiled sires who loyal wept
  By streams of Babylon,
The "Pleasant land" of your desire
  His thoughts did dwell upon.

Till He restored the glory land,
  He had first for you espied;
The sorrow of thy widowed years
  His wrath hath satisfied.

Thy sons no more "Forsaken" art,
  Nor thou termed "Desolate,"
The Lord hath called thee "Beulah" land
  And given thee new estate.

O Palestine and Africa,
  Now stretching forth your hands,
Again thou shalt His glory see,
  As His remembered lands!

"AHAVA"

At Ahava, stream of Persia,
There we halted, fasted, pray'd
That o'er the robber-ridden desert
We might journey unafraid.

On Jehovah, God of battles,
We had rested, trusted, stay'd,
Now, in this, our hour of testing,
Could we seek for lesser aid?

By Ahava, stream of Persia,
Fears were routed, worsted, laid;
For our children, wives and treasure,
God our confidence was made.

From Ahava, stream of Persia,
With no visual guard of men;
But with God's "good hand" upon us
Safe we reached Jerusalem!

THE UNIVERSAL CALL

(Ps. 50:1)

From lands of dawn and rising sun
To where his westering course is run,
There comes to this old, teeming earth,
Thro' cypress shade and scenes of mirth,
     The call of God.

No ear there is so dull but hears,
Somewhere adown the path of years,
The voice that heeds not class nor clan
But finds the longing heart of man—
     The call of God.

More swift than wireless thro' the air,
While suns from morn to evening wear,
This summons comes that bids us rest,
That satisfies the heart's deep quest—
     The call of God.

"THE LEGION OF THE LARK"

"Legion of the Lark," great Caesar called
Those daring men he chose from captive Gaul
To be his body-guard, and follow him
Thro' all his future wars and vict'ries grim;
Because they bore upon their helmets high
The image of that bird of song in upper sky;
For Caesar loved to have those warriors near
Who met the brunt of battle with songs of
    cheer.

His "Legion of the Lark" are soldiers of the
    King,
Who on the moral battlefield know how to
    fight and sing;
Who defeat the Prince of darkness in his most
    subtle ways,
As nothing so appals him as constant prayer
    and praise;
Thus those Christian soldiers, who season
    with a song
Every stern engagement, are God's Legion of
    the strong;

And we may well imagine their sweetest notes
    will come
As a final strain of triumph when they are
    soaring home.

"NOT OTHERWISE"

Into a room where a sick one lay,
    One day her pastor came to pray.
He thought to find the maiden sad,
    And pondered long what words he had
To comfort bring where want and pain
    Had done the work of that dread twain.
" 'Tis hard to bear, I know," he said,
    Taking a seat beside her bed.
She looked at him in pained surprise,
    And spoke, as a light shone in her eyes,
    "I would not have it otherwise."

"Not otherwise! how can you say
    With life now in its opening day?
It must be hard to just lie here—
    Within this room so void of cheer?"
He watched her face in wonder now,
    Such radiance lighted eye and brow;
"Why you, yourself, have often told
    How Christ gives blessings manifold.
I've found it true; in His will lies
    All peace, and leaves no room for sighs;
    I would not have it otherwise!"

The man of God went on his way,
    Hers was the ministry that day;
Within that barren, upper room,
    He'd found his sermons lived at home;
The calm which comes, he'd often said,
    When all is on the altar laid—
Into his house, to think it o'er,

He passed and closed his study door.
There he, too, came to realize
    That this was life's one greatest prize:
    Not to "Have it otherwise."

"THOSE THINGS WHICH ARE BEFORE"

(Phil. 3:13)

"Those things which are before,"
The things that give us wings to soar
In vision to that heavenly land,
Where our Christ reigns at God's right hand,
Blest end of all I seek and preach,
Towards these I reach!

Those things which make the cloudy days,
All bright with special hymns of praise,
That seeing, one doth plainly say,
"I seek a kingdom far away,"
The things that transcend human speech,
Towards these I reach!

"Those things" on high which are before,
Mean climbing days are never o'er;
That as the Old Year's shades are falling,
I upward press to God's "high calling,"
In Christ, the end of all I teach,
Towards Him I reach!

"THAT BREAD OF LIFE"

(Suggested by a Sunday School Lesson on the Giving of Manna)

O Christ, "that bread of life,
 If daily in the strife,
We did but feast on Thee,
 How strong our lives would be!

O Christ, "that Bread of life,
 As doctrines false are rife,
O may our tempters see
 We are faring well on Thee!

They who on manna fed,
 Did eat and they are dead;
Be Thou our souls supply,
 That we may never die!

GOD'S SECRET

(Ps. 25:14)

Precious pacts we have with dear ones,
　　Sweetest things in secret said
Only for the ears of near ones:
　　Hearts that to our hearts are wed.

But sweeter far to those that fear Him
　　Is the secret of the Lord,
Only shared with those most near Him:
　　Hearts with Him in blest accord.

Highest motive to revere Him:
　　That His life for ours was spent;
Just because He'd have us near Him
　　Wide the temple veil was rent!

OMNIPOTENCE

A whole Red Sea
Is quite impassable to you and me;
But God's power at man's impossible starts,
And, lo, each Red Sea He divides in parts!

CHRIST'S ACQUAINTANCESHIP

He to the sad and sorrow-worn
    Affords a swift and sure relief,
Because He, who hath our nature borne,
    Acquainted was with grief.

One thing, howe'er, was never writ
    In that Book—our fondest treasure—
That He, who is the source of it,
    Acquainted was with pleasure!

A PRAYER

Use me, Lord, use me for my race,
To send their status up a pace;
To make their merits better known;
Hasten their coming to their own!

Use me, Lord, use me for Thy Church,
May lost ones never vainly search
For the glow of my small light
Out upon the world's dark night!

Use me, Lord, use for Thyself alone,
The life that's ransom'd by Thine own;
May it a living letter be—
With a message straight from Thee!

"NO MORE SEA"

**(Suggested by a poem in the Literary Digest,
regretting the absence of the sea
from heaven)**

"There shall be no more sea,"
For endless sorrow rests
Upon its ever-heaving crests;
In that land where many mansions be,
Sorrow and sighing away shall flee,
   There could be "no more sea."

"There shall be no more sea,"
For the wicked are like its troubled waves,
Whom nothing quiets, nothing saves;
In that realm where all is melody,
And peace as a river flows on in majesty,
   There can be no more sea!

"There shall be no more sea!"
The sea divides, and causes salt, salt tears;
Begets forebodings and unbidden fears;
There souls exult; no partings know, nor
   sighs,
As God doth wipe away all tears from our
   eyes.
   "There shall be no more sea!"

"There shall be no more sea!"
I am glad this word was said—
The sea shall cease to be when it gives up
   its dead!

For when we are transplanted to that home
    above,
There'll only be one ocean—the ocean of God's
    love!

"UNREST"

They tell us there's unrest today,
That men grope blindly for the Way;
That the price we've paid for liberty
Is a world-drifting "all at sea."

They tell us that old truths are dead;
That the last word has not been said;
Love's waxen cold and faith diminished;
So we've forgotten: 'It is finished.'

Tell, tell us (but it is not so),
That men know not the way to go;
For still there's Christ and Calvary,
The Risen One, saying: "Come unto me."

Though times may change, the Truth endures,
And Christ's touch still man's fever cures;
And still He calls to rest and peace;
He breaks the bow, makes wars to cease.

No talk of "change" must faith dissever,
Since Christ's the same "today, forever,"
Our yesterdays—lived in His name—
Still point the path to deathless fame.

"THE OLD PATHS"

(Jer. 6:16)

Those old lov'd paths across the scented fields,
Where we so lightly trod the well-worn way,
Inhaling fragrance of the new-mown hay,
Or perfume which the sweet white clover
    yields;
Till scent of hay and clover magic wields
And visions new each care-free, happy day,
When papa's loving hand-clasp seem'd to say:
Here's all the shelter of a thousand shields!
Those ancient paths, anent the seer's behest,
As he, while streaming tears his eyes o'erfill,
Bade Israel forsake her wayward quest,
Bear they a likeness to these ways of rest?
It must be so, for we are children still,
And those "old paths" our Heavenly Father's
    will.

FESTIVAL DAYS

THE NEW YEAR AND SONG

Start the New Year singing,
Keep God's praises ringing,
Cheer to sad hearts bringing;
Start the New Year singing!

Start the New Year singing,
Keep Hope's pinions winging,
Wide the glad notes flinging;
Start the New Year singing!

Start the New Year singing,
To the old tunes clinging,
They with grace are ringing:
Start the New Year singing!

Start the New Year singing,
Song is faith upspringing,
Victory's gates outswinging;
Start the New Year singing!

FACING THE FUTURE

(Isa. 55:12)

As we life's journey tread,
Though mountains loom ahead,
We need not faint nor fear,
For the hills shall disappear;
Lo, as we onward march along,
We'll find them cleft with song!

THE NEW YEAR

What a word is this for the glad New Year,
To send us forth with a heart of cheer!
We shall place our regnant banners here:
"The set of their faces was forward!"

The year spreads out as an open book,
There is no time for a backward look;
We've closed the account, a reck'ning took—
The set of our faces is forward.

There's an upward path and a shining way,
A light that falls from the King of day,
And we shall win in the battle's fray,
The set of our faces is forward!

THE MESSAGE OF EASTER

In the gray down of Easter morn,
Joy to the world was newly born;
In the empty tomb and riven gloom
Sprang Hope—a Star-to earth illume.

In the low word which Mary stirred,
Such magic rang that we have heard;
Our names He calls and on us falls
The rapture that our lives enthralls.

Death's chain is broken, to us the token
Then to the women sweetly spoken;
The night is o'er, He goeth before;
Go spread the news from shore to shore.

By lives of light, show forth the might
That broke the pow'r of Death that night;
Give every soul by sin imprison'd
A chance to know that Christ has risen!

"BECAUSE HE LIVES"

As by the death of Him who was
   Holy and undefiled,
We to the Maker of mankind
   Have now been reconciled,
Much more, then, by His risen life,
   Which He so freely gives,
We here are conquerors in the strife;
   We live because He lives.

As by the path of death He went
   Fearless and undismayed,
We, too, within our narrow house
   May trustingly be laid;
For there we shall not long abide,
   Because He ever lives,
We shall rise upward to His side
   In the new life He gives.

"CHILDREN OF THE RESURRECTION"

(Luke 20:36)

A name all permeate with power
And beauteous as hte Easter flower,
Is that, we read, is on them called
Who're counted worthy of that world,
Rich blossom of their earth selection:
 "Children of the resurrection."

Who dropp'd, with flesh, the ways of men
And rose with Him to live again—
Lives pure as holy angels are,
Sans spot, or wrinkle or a flaw,
By seal divine is their election:
 "Children of the resurrection."

Offsprings, they, upon whose brow
Death's shadow never cometh now.
Of earth, once mortals' paths they trod,
Of heaven, now the sons of God,
Theirs is for aye the life perfection:
 "Children of the resurrection."

"THERE WAS DARKNESS"

The earth is bright today,
Because Christ went the way
    Of Calvary.
The gloom and darkness there
Have made the whole earth fair.

On us God's face doth shine
Because 'twas hid from Thine
    On Calvary.
Out of Thy three hours' night
Has come our grace of light!

THE CHILDREN'S HOSANNAS

Christ loved their guileless praise
    And would not them deny;
King of the hearts of men, He knew
    They would not change their cry:
Today, hosannas on their tongues,
    The next, "Away to die!"

Christ heard and spake to those
    Who'd chide their joyous ways,
"Have ye not read 'tis said of old,
    In David's tuneful lays,
That God hath chosen such as these
    To set forth perfect praise?"

Christ knew Earth understood
    The children's happy chorus;
And said that had they silent been,
    The stones had spoken for us!
Oh, may we never hold our peace,
    When the Spirit stealeth o'er us!

THE FIRST EASTER MORNING

I'm glad that women linger'd longest
  Where "they crucified Him."
I'm glad their love was true and strongest
  That they ne'er denied Him!

I'm glad that three of them were first
  At day's faint dawning,
To find that He death's chains had burst
  On earth's first Easter morning!

I'm glad it was a woman's name
  Held His first greeting;
When Mary to the garden came—
  Oh, that wondrous meeting!

THANKSGIVING

Every day, if praise be given,
Contains a little bit of heaven;
Every day if met with cheer,
Is just "the best day of the year."

Each hath given its full share
Towards the harvests rich and fair;
Each has kept, in tears or mirth,
God's ancient covenant with earth.

A twelvemonth of such wealthy days
Merits the Nation's song of praise;
Calls each soul to come away
And joyful keep Thanksgiving Day.

To quit the busy paths we've trod,
And spend at least one day with God,
Who says, My habitat with Israel
Is in the place where praises dwell.

OUR SOURCE OF STRENGTH

To live the whole year's busy length,
    And at its close stand with the strong,
    Upon our lips the victor's song,
God's joy must be our 'biding strength.

It sings in all the ripened grain,
    Our golden fields from east to west,

With flocks and harvests richly blest,
Are bars of His great triumph strain.

It wells in every battle fought,
  (By tongue or pen, or by the sword,
  That nations may with right accord)
Which has for lasting progress wrought.

But finds its fullest, highest chord
  In those who, following His ways,
  Have made their lives a psalm of praise,
As daily walked they with their Lord!

Thus our whole great nation's strength
  Lies in the things of God's delight:
  In Mercy, Justice, Truth and Right,
Throughout her breadth and border's length.

WHEN THE HEART KEEPS CHRISTMAS

Still there shines that glory light,
Which made the skies so passing bright
Upon that far-off Holy Night,
    When the heart keeps Christmas.

Still unto our Lord and King,
We, as the Wise Men, haste to bring
Our costliest and most precious thing,
    When the heart keeps Christmas.

Still to all who 'round us dwell.
With glad and reverent lips we tell
The tidings of "Emanuel"—
    When the heart keeps Christmas.

THE HEART OF CHRISTMAS

'Twere sad indeed at Christmas time,
With all the sleigh-bells' merry chime,
The auto's noisy puff and gong,
To fail to catch the angel's song.

But sadder still to have our eyes
So chained to what about us lies:
To raise them not for the vision higher,
The radiance of that heavenly choir.

Saddest, if seeking here and there
For Christmas bargains cheap and rare;
For gifts to make our fellow men,
We miss the road to Bethlehem.

For then, indeed, the hymn would cease
Ere we had caught its note of Peace;
And, missing the chant, the sight sublime,
We'd lose the heart of Christmas-time.

MARY'S PART

To the shepherds came the music
　Of that seraphic angel throng,
That made the plains of Bethlehem
　Reverberate with their song.
Theirs, too, was the joy of seeing,
　When the angels had gone away,
The Babe, who, as 'twas told them,
　In a lowly manger lay.
But, more blest than outward vision,
　Or the rustle of angel wings,
Is that word one said of Mary:
　She ponder'd and "kept these things."

For the sweetest song hath ending,
And the vision will not stay;
　But the gain of once-heard music
　Lies just in Mary's way.
To the inner ear of the Spirit
　Will come that wondrous song,
And its words of joy and comfort
　Their bliss for aye prolong
Thro' the common days that follow
　'Midst cold traffic's busy mart,
If our is the stored-up treasure
　And Mary's pondering part.

GOD'S GIFT

Oh, friends, who also have started
  On the road to the City of Light,
Let us keep, in rapture, clear-hearted,
  The memory of that "Holy Night."
When a Saviour to mortals was given;
  When the clouds with joy were riven
As the heavenly visitants came,
  Out of a brightness aflame,
To make known the infant's name;
And all Earth's corners to fill
With peace to men and good will!
  Aye, these are the things in December,
We love, best of all, to remember.
  May we never from their anchorage drift,
But keep fast hold of God's Gift!

MISCELLANEOUS

ROBERT BROWNING

(May 7, 1912; born May 7, 1812)

The Joy that sees the roses,
    Jeweled with heavenly dew;
The bloom that May discloses,
    Beauteous for me and you;

The Love that's lyric-human,
    Euterpe's rarest wine,
That fiinds its "Star" in woman,
    Its Christ, the One Divine;

The Faith that walks "breast forward,"
    Bouyantly the emerald sod;
That meets Death as no coward,
    Clear-eyed, so "sure of God";

Are ours because one morning,
    A century's flight away,
To earth came Robert Browning,
    In the "blossom month" of May.

THE CLUB WOMAN

Hers to fill the vacant place
    And do the thing that none else sees;
To all life's vexing problems face
    And many an unfair burden ease;

To stand beside the working girl,
    And all who, silent, suffer wrong;
To soften commerce's busy whirl
    With just a little bit of song;

To be in home, in church and state
    A power that ever makes for good,
Whose purpose is to elevate
    And nobler make all womanhood;

To so enlarge the mind and eye
    That life, tho' immanent with Duty,
Over it the humblest may descry
    The perfect rainbow arc of Beauty;

To have it broadly understood,
    Thro' ways that seem but purely human,
That naught which makes for sisterhood
    Is foreign to the true club woman.

ROBIN REDBREAST

(Written for a little child)

Robin Redbreast the other day
Came with merry notes to say:
"Winter's snow has gone away."
He lighted on my garden fence,
And twittered cheerily from thence;
So glad was he that it was Spring,
He couldn't tarry long to sing,
But soon again was on the wing;
For, having news so very good,
He flew to tell the neighborhood;
While I was very glad that he
Had cheered me with his company;
That sight of him I had not miss'd,
Being on Red Robin's calling list!

ANNIVERSARY SONG

TUNE: "Battle Hymn of the Republic."

(Written for and sung at Detroit Y. W. C. A.
February, 1916.)

To-day we have a sisterhood that wide its flag
    unfurls,
And sends afar its bugle note to ever-widening
    worlds,
Because fifty years ago there was some one
    who thought of girls!
We girls are marching on.

CHORUS:
    Praise Jehovah for our founders!
    Praise Jehovah for our founders!
    Praise Jehovah for our founders!
    We girls are marching on!

To shield them from the Tempter who so swift
    his arrow hurls,
And daily seeks to them engulf in follies' madd-
    'ning whirls,
Just fifty years ago there was some one who
    thought of girls!
We girls are marching on!

To show those hours have enterprise that're
    girt with song of merles,
To teach them how to work aright and seek all
    goodly pearls,
Just fifty years ago this month somebody
    thought of girls!
We girls are marching on!

ANNIVERSARY HYMN*

TUNE: "How Sweet the Name of Jesus
Sounds."

We meet within this sacred place,
  Rich with our hopes and fears,
Glad sons of Ethiopia's race,
  To mark a hundred years.

Since Allen, our great founder, stood
  On that historic day,
For Christ and human brotherhood
  To all who own His sway.

Thro' fire and flood and slav'ry's night,
  Within a weary land,
Our Zion proved a beacon light,
  Her priests a helping hand.

So beautiful their rev'rent feet,
  As they the Gospel spread,
'Tis ours to catch its martial beat,
  The music of their tread!

To-day upon this hallowed ground,
  To crown our jubilee,
We'd own, with fervor newly found,
  The Man of Galilee!

*Written in honor of the 100th Anniversary of the
founding of the African Methodist Episcopal Church
by Richard Allen, at Philadelphia, 1816.

OUR TERCENTENARY

(1620-1920)

Three wonder-holden centuries have flown
Since first we claimed this country as our own;
O, Spirit Divine, we pray Thee on us come,
Forbid that they should pass us silent, dumb;
But may we see, as writ in living fire,
Some thrilling word that shall all hearts in-
 spire
Thrown 'cross the scroll of each one hundred
 years,
Which mark a Nation's growth—its hopes and
 fears,
To fittingly epitomize and vocal make
These bygone centuries—a torch to onward
 take!

This trinity of cycles, we reverently would say
First, shows us God the Father who led the
 Pilgrims all the way
As they in work and worship as comrades
 bravely stood,
We read its living message in the great word—
 BROTHERHOOD!
Then seeing God, the Son, who truly makes
 men free,
With pen immersed in crimson we spelled out
 LIBERTY!
The closing of the triad brings us to this hour
And with awed gaze we read the Spirit's gift
 of POWER!

Yet, God of our fathers, we cannot fully cele-
    brate
Until we know this land once more is conse-
    crate
To God, the Father of us all,
To the Anointed One, who knows no great and
    no small.
And to the Holy Ghost who would send us
    onward from this hour,
A mighty nation—clothed with living Power.

" THE WINGS OF THE MORNING."

They are pinions zepher blown
From some far-off seraph zone;
They are unseen ships of air,
That will waft us otherwhere.

They are cherub chariots free
To the utmost paths of sea,
Waiting each diurnal round
On our Fancy "outward bound."

A WINTER PICTURE

Oh, the sunlight on the snow!
And the little twigs aglow!
Thro' the wooing of Jack Frost
All uncomeliness is lost,
When a winter morning's sun
Smiles on what the night has done.

Oh, the sunlight on the snow!
And the barren shrubs aglow!
'Tis a beauty close at hand,
For the parks are fairyland,
And trees yester'eve so bare
Now crystal pennants wear!

Oh, pity those who do not know
The charm of sunlight on the snow;
Whose sun-kiss'd eyes have never seen
The trees in all their wintry sheen!

ANNIVERSARY HYMN

(Celebrating the 80th Anniversary of the
founding of Bethel A. M. E. Church, De-
troit, Michigan, May 29, 1921.)

TUNE: "Federal Street, L. M."

When we reflect on all God's ways,
  His dealings with our Zion here,
We can but lift our hearts in praise
  For blessings on each passing year.

For all the countless deeds of love,
  For victories His grace hath brought,
We grateful lift our eyes above
  And humbly cry, "What hath God wrought!"

For eighty years our Bethel's kept
  The faith, once given to the saints,
Spotless and pure, though oft she's wept,
  And upward sent her tears and plaints.

From small beginnings we have grown,
  From days of debt and hours of stress,
Till lo! we now this temple own,
  And here two thousand Christ confess!

We thank God that He keeps her still,
  And calls this Bethel—House of God;
With forward look to do Thy will
  We follow where our fathers trod!

"SCHOOL, DRIVE SLOWLY."

A little sign in white and red,
  Designed and set most duly,
To check autoists, speeding ahead,
  Reads: "School, drive slowly."

That little ones to daily tasks
  May safely go and wholly,
The City warns and frequent asks
  This: "School, drive slowly."

A little sign, when thought controls,
  Is writ 'cross life most truly:
Lest injury should hap to souls,
  Heed: "School, drive slowly."

LOST—OUR LITTLE GIRLS

What's become of little girls
  Who used to wear such pretty dresses,
That they've lost all but their curls—
  And loss of these ofttimes distresses?

What's become of little girls?
  They don't look dainty any more;
So early shaped to fashion's whirls,
  They'll ne'er be women at the core!

When you see the tots at play,
  Which is Sally, which is Jim?
For your life you couldn't say,
  Though your eyesight isn't dim.

O, Dame Fashion, keep your sway,
  If you must, 'mid social whirls;
But restore Ye Olden Day—
  Give us back our little girls!

OUR FLAG

(June 14, 1777, to June 14, 1914)

Banner of our country's magnificent domain,
We hail thy anniversary that comes to us
    again!
Proudly we review these one hundred and odd
    years
Since at a cost unreckon'd of precious blood
    and tears,
Liberty and Right proclaimed their sovran
    sway,
And, sweeping the might of crowned heads
    away,
Unfurled a new Republic's sacred ensign here,
And lit the lamp of Progress on this western
    hemisphere.

Flag that proudly waves from east to western
    sea,
Thrice baptized in crimson by thy passion to
    be free!
Thine ideal a nation where all men equal are,
And each is reprsented in his state's resplend-
    ent star.
Oh, still this soil is hallow'd long as thy starry
    folds
Wave grandly over veterans of the days that
    tried men's souls;
To-day before a patriot would see thy laurel's
    less,

He to the steel of conflict would bare his
    loyal breast;
In this high expectation which doth each bo-
    som thrill—
That all "thy ancient glory shall play about
    thee still!"

THE SYMBOL OF THE RED CROSS

They've hungry children fed
Where bullets terror spread,
That's why their cross is red!

Their steps in mercy led
Where human blood was shed,
That's why their cross is red!

They've words of comfort sped
To souls to sorrow wed,
That's why their cross is red!

They've the glad Evangel read
Beside the soldier's bed,
That's why their cross is red!

"To serve," I came, Christ said,
He who on Calvary bled;
That's why their cross is red!

A WAR-TIME PRAYER—1917.

Father, in heaven, Thy purposes prove,
Through the dark shadows, may we feel Thy
love!
Christ, our Redeemer, who alone sets men free,
Guide, guard our soldiers, who cross the blue
sea!
Tried in war's furnace, may the fires refine;
Called on to suffer, may we not repine;
Purg'd of our vanity, shorn of our pride;
Out from the trenches, we'd rise purified;
Let democracy's triumph, distinctions efface,
All men be brothers, regardless of race!

THE SOURCE OF WARS

(James 4:1)

"Whence come wars?" the apostle cries,
  In eager wish to set men's eyes
On those secret hidden things
  From which trouble constant springs.

Come they not, as flame from embers,
  From those lusts within your members?
Hidden far from human gaze,
  In your hearts, there starts the blaze.

Covetings of another's wealth,
   Desire to take his land by stealth,
Marshal hosts no gas nor high grenade
   With strength to kill hath e'er been made.

Church of God, just here's your place;
   War's not vanquish'd save by grace;
If you would "leadership" maintain,
   Tell the OLD STORY o'er again!

WHEN THE HEART KEEPS CHRISTMAS

Still there shines that glory light,
Which made the skies so passing bright
Upon that far-off Holy Night,
   When the heart keeps Christmas.

Still unto our Lord and King,
We, as the Wise Men, haste to bring
Our costliest and most precious thing,
   When the heart keeps Christmas.

Still to all who 'round us dwell,
With glad and reverent lips we tell
The tidings of "Emanuel,"—
   When the heart keeps Christmas.

Garden of Memories

BY

MAZIE EARHART CLARK

"We all have a Garden of Memories
As deep as the heart of a rose."

DEDICATED

TO

MY FRIENDS

IN MEMORY OF

MY HUSBAND

SGT. GEORGE J. CLARK

WHO PASSED AWAY MAY 31, 1919.

"He was a man, take him for all in all,
I shall not look upon his like again."

My thanks are tendered to those who helped me in the compilation of this verse, and especially do I want to mention my friend, JANE HECK whose encouragement and sympathetic understanding have meant much to me.

EATON PUBLISHING COMPANY
Cincinnati, Ohio

FOREWORD

I have been moved to publish this book of verse, dedicated to "My Friends", in the hope and belief that the simple philosophy of the thoughts expressed herein may prove comforting and stimulating to anyone in need of encouragement—just as was I after the death of my husband.

While my husband lived his protecting love and encouragement were stimulants which inspired me to attempt many things. After his passing, it was as though I had reached the cross-roads in life,—I seemed to have run up a blind ally, where one cannot see what lies head, and is afraid to go on. For a while I seemed to have lost the ability to live courageously; life seemed to stretch emptily and endlessly ahead of me.

In looking back, however, I find that I dwelt in this "Slough of Despond" only so long as I was thinking of my husband as "dead". The moment my mind grasped the fact, and clung to it tenaciously, that he was not dead, but was truly "Just Away," and that his love was stronger than death, all my waning faith and courage returned to me, and I found myself soothed and comforted by the strength of his guiding hand,—that hand that was held out to me just as strongly after death as it had been in life. And thus it was that I realized that what is written into one's own life dies with one, but what one has written into the lives of others lives on in his inheritors.

And thus it is, from my own observation and experience, that I say to you, dear friends, that it is not necessary for any of us to end our journey in a blind alley. We can always GO ON. And that is why I wanted to publish this book,—not only as a testimonial to my husband, which it is, but also believing that a word of encouragement, from a person who has lived fully and suffered, can help one to find the right road. And because many persons have been kind enough to say that my outlook appears to them wholesome and helpful, I hope that I have said something which will be of service to others.

MAZIE EARHART CLARK.

GARDEN OF MEMORIES

MY GARDEN OF MEMORIES

In the soul lies the garden of memories
  Shielded from prying eyes
And there sitting in solitude
  Sweet thoughts of the past arise.
Golden hours that are cherished
  Tho' love has grown dim and low
There's a fragrance in the garden
  That leaves my heart aglow.

No one enters my garden of memories
  Save he who holds the key to my heart,
And we two enjoy the fragrance
  That its sweetness doth impart.
You too have a garden of memories,
  As deep as the heart of a rose,
Where you may enter whenever you feel
  The need of tranquil repose.

| 7 |

MY DREAM BOY

There's a secret I'd never tell
  And this one I have kept so well
That not even you, my Dream Boy
  Knew of the happiness and joy
Your presence brought
  And no others have I sought
For I found all I desired in
  My Dream Boy.

And now that you are far away
  From me both night and day,
Sweet memories will remain
  To soothe my heart's pain.
I know you will always be true to me
  And love me with sincerity
That is your love for me
  My Dream Boy.

Thru the silent night I lie awake,
  Wishing sweetheart for your dear sake
That my spirit could rush thru the air
  And banish every fretful care.
You would lay your head upon my breast;
  I would share your burden and bring you rest
My Dream Boy.

The secret I am telling you is sweet
  And when we meet I will thrice repeat;
Watch the lovelight in your eyes
  As unfathomable as wide spreading skies.
We'll be happy our hearts so free
  We'll wander through purple shadows
Just you and me
  My Dream Boy.

Along our path we have found the roses,
  Wild flowers and beautiful posies
Grass like emeralds and the azure sky
  And zephyr winds bidding us goodbye.
To give way to the wintery blast
  Like the joy in our lives it cannot last
My Dream Boy.

Don't forget God watches over thee
  And if it is His will you'll soon be free
Then we'll be happy once again
  And your sweetheart will gladly reign
In your heart of all hearts my dear
  There will be naught to fear
Because we'll be together
  My Dream Boy.

[8]

UNFURL, THE FLAG

Unfurl the flag, all ye nations,
    Let them wave in every land;
Show true patriotic spirit,
    For the men who fought so grand.

Remove your hats, do them honor,
    They sacrificed life and home;
To retrieve their country's standard,
    Under God's starry dome.

They were men of might and sinew;
    Not the quaking, trembling kind;
That marched off to do their duty
    For the loved ones left behind.

Though we strew their graves with flowers,
    With tender hands and loving care,
And though our hearts were filled with anguish,
    Still we needs must leave them there.

In the ground that's been made sacred,
    By the shedding of their blood;
On the cruel field of battle,
    Relentless as a seething flood.

Their names are now emblazoned,
    On a tablet beyond the sky,
The Captain there will lead them
    Through the Golden Gates on high.

Their fame will be resounded,
    By the vast Heavenly Throng;
Singing "Onward Christian Soldiers"
    As they march along.

ARMISTICE DAY

Our hearts are filled with sadness,
  And tears bedim our eyes,
There seems to be a grayness
  In the erstwhile azure skies.

Our minds revert to Flanders Field,
  Where the red, red poppies grow;
Where tombstones tell the story,
  Gleaming white as snow.

And in this silent city,
  Lay men who gave their all;
Who suffered untold agony,
  Obeying their country's call.

When asked for reinforcements,
  To strengthen the ranks, of France,
Our men marched bravely onward,
  Without a backward glance.

Our sorrows are universal,
  We weep not alone,
There are many hearts aching,
  For the men who marched from home.

But the U. S. A. feels almost sure,
  That Peace has come to stay,
Thru the help of our dear soldier boys,
  That we honor thus today.

———

VESPERS

(Dedicated to Mrs. Ann. Howard Matthews)

While walking in the twilight
  I heard the sweetest strain;
It was the evening vespers;
  They were singing a soft refrain.

The organist seemed inspired;
  Such chords I never heard before;
Her face wore the look of an angel;
  Spellbound I stood at the door.

I was drawn inside as by magic,
  But there was not an empty seat;
I stood with tears freely falling
  As with the rest I did repeat—

Holy, holy, holy, Lord God Almighty,
  Never forsake us, be our shield;
Holy, holy, Father above us,
  Be our protection, hear our appeal.

And from that evening I was found
  Within some sacred wall
Listening to the teaching
  Of Christ who had died for all.

[10]

MY PRAYER

Jesus, be with me every hour
Thou Precious Lamb of God,
Shield me from temptation
Wield thy chastening rod.
Create in me a heart that's true
For my fellow man,
And if I lay me down to sleep
And life should reach its span,
May this prayer live on and on
Even tho my life is o'er
May it help some weary one
To reach the celestial shore.
Send the Holy Ghost I pray
To purify me within,
Create in me a clean heart Oh God
And wash away my sin.

ARE YOU LONESOME?

I'm as lonesome as I can be,
    Since you bade me goodbye;
My heart aches just for you dear,
    And the winds with me sigh.
You told me that you loved me,
    And that you'd always be true,
But you went away, so far away,
    Left me sad and blue.

I wonder if you feel lonesome, dear,
    And yearn to see me too,
Tell me you really love me,
    And that you sometimes feel blue;
Down in the garden of roses dear,
    Where we vowed we'd be true,
It is there you'll find me waiting,
    Waiting sweetheart for you.

CHORUS

I never knew how lonesome,
    Your going would make me feel,
But it made me so awfully lonesome,
    My heart makes this appeal—
Come back and I'll be waiting,
    In the rose garden 'neath the moon,
Come back and I'll be waiting,
    Yearning to see you soon.

[11]

A CARESS

A caress, soft as thistle down,
  Came on the wings of a breeze.
As I sat in meditation,
  Watching the falling leaves.
There hovered 'round and about me
  A perfume rare and sweet,
Wafted up from the roses
  Growing at my feet.

I raised the blood-red roses,
  And caressed them in return,
Bestowing on them the essence of love,
  That within my heart did burn.
Within their perfumed sweetness.
  A message I found for me,
From one who, although silent,
  Still loves me tenderly.

SMILE WITH ME

Don't bid farewell to the sunshine,
  Don't bid farewell to the rain;
Why make your life one of sadness?
  The clouds will turn silver again.
Keep your heart happy and smile;
  It will help you, just try it and see;
When the clouds that were dark are all silver,
  Then remember to smile with me.

Think of the mothers and fathers
  Who lost all they ever held dear;
A smile and a kind word will help them;
  Be a comfort while you are here.
The world with its sorrows and troubles
  Has burdens enough, can't you see?
So help all you can, someone needs you,
  But remember to smile with me.

Smile when the sun is shining,
  Smile when the rains appear,
Smile when your friends forsake you,
  Smile—let not your thoughts be drear:
Smile, there are hearts that are aching;
  Your smile may help them to see
The cloud with its silvery lining,
  And then you will smile with me.

THE RAINBOW TRAIL

My girl lives in the Golden West
  At the end of the Rainbow Trail,
And there she's as true as the skies of blue,
  And her love will never fail.
When she went away I heard her say,
  "I know you'll be coming soon;"
So I'll meet her there, my sweetheart fair,
  And we'll go on our honeymoon.

Chorus

I long to hear the hum of the train,
  As it speeds over the shining rail
To the Golden West and the girl I love best
  At the end of the Rainbow Trail.

When I think of my dear Pal,
  It makes me feel so blue
To have her away from me a day—
  I know she is lonesome too.
So I'm going away, I'll start today,
  Through storm, through wind and hail,
To greet the one that I love best
  At the end of the Rainbow Trail.

DRIFTING

Drifting slowly down the stream,
  'Neath the pale moonlight;
Drifting into lands of dreams
  Into perfect delight.
Gliding 'neath the star-lit sky,
  Just you and I,
Peeping through the bower green
  As the moments swiftly fly.

When the shifting clouds appear,
  And evening shadows fall,
I will always be near you,
  In answer to your call.
I will gently hold your hand,
  And caress you, too,
As we drift to lands unknown,
  Because I love just you

Chorus:

Drifting, drifting down the stream,
  Just you and I,
As over us the bright stars gleam
  From the purple sky.
All the world seems fast asleep
  In this mystic hour;
The fragrance of roses sweet
  From the mossy bower.

BROTHERHOOD OF MANKIND

Great is the soul of mankind,
  And noble are men's deeds,
So keen are their perceptive powers
  To see each other's needs.
Like brothers they take their stand,
  To help those in distress,
To build a brighter future,
  And find true happiness.

This brotherhood of mankind.
  Is known throughout the land,
And you'll always find them ready
  To lend a helping hand.
Conditions are appalling;
  Man seeks his daily bread,
Without work or help in sight
  He wishes he were dead.

His dear ones wait and wonder
  Why he does not bring them food,
Ho walks the street, bemoans his fate,
  In a sad and mournful mood.
As he walks, he scans each face,
  Some young, but lined with care,
Others happy, heedless, selfish,
  Would not of their abundance share.

He knew not which way to turn
  In his days of dark distress
Should he go home with empty hands.
  They would all be sure to guess.
They'd know conditions had not changed,
  That he had met his Waterloo,
He cannot beg, he would not steal.
  Discouraged, oh, what shall he do.

Just then he felt a gentle touch,
  Then a mild and sincere voice,
Thank God, at last he's found a friend,
  And has cause to rejoice.
It was through untiring efforts
  Of those who are doing good,
Those who have goodness at heart,
  Known as the Brotherhood.

May God protect them all,
  And share with them His love,
Fill them with His Spirit Divine,
  Through the Holy Ghost above.
And when He comes to judge the world,
  The quick and the dead,
May the Brotherhood's starry crown
  Shine like diamonds on each head.

[14]

THE MASTER AND HIS VIOLIN

This violin of rosewood,
  Once played active parts,
In many thousand concerts,
  And on the strings of many hearts.
It has caused tears unbidden
  To gush from saddened eyes,
It has been the inspiration
  For deeds that never die.

It's vibratory sweetness
  Was of such one could not forget,
It will linger on through countless years,
  And it's silence brings regret.
In ecstasy one could listen,
  Enthralled within his heart,
As the master on this violin
  Played with such skill and art.

He lived not in the present,
  He just relieved the past,
He knew his days were numbered,
  Each rhapsody perhaps his last.
He could not see the faces,
  They're lost, as in a mist to him,
His soul so steeped in the music,
  Transmitted through his violin.

[15]

HER LOST VALENTINE

Dan Cupid, Dan Cupid
  Get on the line,
Someone has lost
  Her dear valentine.
She rang up this morning
  And said hello,
Asked how can I find him
  In voice soft and low.

I said that I'd try
  My method was brief,
For my duty she'll find
  Is to drive away grief.
That's why I'm calling
  On you, friend of mine,
Because of your luck
  In bringing sunshine.

These two had vowed
  That they'd never part,
When you shot the arrow
  That pierced through their hearts.
Call the broadcasting station
  Get on the line,
Send out a message
  To her lost valentine.

DOCTOR DAN CUPID

A man in front of a looking glass
  Was arranging a vexing tie,
A maid stood by a little stream
  And softly breathed a sigh.

Cupid lingered not far away
  And knew these hearts were sad,
So he brought these two together
  And now two hearts are glad.

SEND THIS ARROW

I know you are not my sweetheart
  But that don't hinder me,
From whispering softly in your ear
  That I would like to be.

[16]

AUTUMN LEAVES

Autumn, with its chilly winds
   Scatter the leaves just everwhere,
Tho clouds are gray and purplê
   The trees are stark and bare.
Leaves of bright and rosy hue
   Mingle with the gold,
The brown and the cardinal
   All 'neath the snow will mold.

They are all of varied color
   And now tossed by the breeze,
They look like many colored lights
   Dropping from the trees.
They're crimson and they're russet
   And some burnished gold,
The artist loves to paint them
   And their beauty hold.

AT THE END OF THE TRAIL

When our trail of life is ended
   Under life's leaden sky,
Where will the pathway lead us
   As the weeping willows sigh.
It may be on the mountain top
   Or down in the valley below,
Where Man and beast have fallen
   And fast deep waters flow.

It may be among the roses
   Whose perfume fills the air,
Or it may lead thru the forest
   Verdant with mosses rare.
It may lead to the ocean
   Where waves are tossed to foam,
Or it may end in a little hut
   That someone calls his home.

It matters not where it leads
   Nor how far away the end,
There is a trail, a long long trail
   Where our earthly time we spend.
Sow it with deeds of kindness
   Tho' up and down you go,
Be careful not to stumble
   When the sun is sinking low.

For when your journey's ended
   You'll find awaiting you,
The fate that you, yourselves, have made
   Step by step as you passed through,
So choose well the path you follow
   For so much on that depends,
For the seeds you sow are the seeds you'll reap
   When your trail of life shall end.

[17]

A HAPPY NEW YEAR

Father Time stands trembling,
With sickle in hand;
He'll soon close his record
All over the land.
Decrepit and old,
He'll vanish from view,
And in his stead
We'll welcome the new.

Father Times takes with him
Memories of gold,
Hearts filled with anguish,
Stories untold.
Our memories we'll place
In a jar with a rose
There to remain
In silent repose.

And may the new record
Be free from strife,
And may fate decree
A harmonious life.
So with faces beaming
We'll join with you,
Watch out the Old Year
And ring in the New.

HOSANNA IN THE HIGHEST

Hosanna, Hosanna, let the joy bells ring
Hosanna, Hosanna, let men and angels sing,
Peace, Peace be unto all
May the blessing on you fall
This beautiful Christmas morn
When for us all a Savior's born.
Hosanna, Hosanna, let men and angels sing.

Hosanna, Hosanna, glad tidings are on the wing,
Hosanna, Hosanna, we crown him new born King,
It is the Father's Holy Plan
To send to us this righteous Man
Who'll teach us of spirtual birth
And bring happiness to fill the earth.
Hosanna, Hosanna, crown Him new born King.

Hosanna, Hosanna, beamed the morning star
Hosanna, Hosanna, that led wise men from afar,
To where our gentle Savior lay
Who came to wash our sins away
And while the host so sweetly sing
We'll hail Him Our Lord and King.
Hosanna, Hosanna, while men and angels sing.

[18]

COMMON CLAY
OR
ADAM AND EVE

God gave unto Adam a Garden,
    With flowers sweet and rare,
And with its great commodities,
    'Twould be hard to compare;
He gave unto his keeping,
    The beast of the field and land,
And dominion over everything,
    Was his but to command.

Adam often walked thru the Garden,
    Viewing the land and the trees,
And would say, "Oh, how wonderful!"
    As his brow was fanned by the breeze;
But, alas! I have no one to talk to,
    I'll ask God to alter His plan,
I feel the need of companionship,
    After all, I'm only a man.

God caused him to fall into slumber,
    Then He took a rib from his side,
And from it made a woman,
    Thus giving Adam a bride;
And Eve, she was fair and beautiful,
    Eclipsing the Evening Star,
Adam gazed at her in wonderment,
    Worshiping her from afar.

Then came the wily serpent,
    To change everything in the plan,
Bringing sorrow into Paradise,
    For this woman and man;
They were no longer happy,
    Eve tempted him and they fell,
She clung with her arms around Adam,
    Trying to cast off the spell.

But God sent His avenging angel,
    With a curved and flaming sword,
They were driven from the Garden,
    For disobeying His word;
From that day man's hardships,
    Would be more than he could bear,
If it were not for the Savior's love,
    Who came that he might share

The brunt of the world's great burdens,
    That had fallen on Adam and Eve;
If baptized in the Water of Life,
    Saved are all who on him believe.
And we are just like Adam,
    Walking in our Gardens today,
We'd not do the things we are doing,
    Were we not made of Common Clay.

[19]

MY DREAM SHIP
FROM THE LAND OF MAKE BELIEVE

My ship has left its harbor
  And is sailing straight to me,
Back from treasure island
  Now its churning the briny sea.
My ship will gladden many
  Even those who have suffered pain,
For they'll soon forget their misery
  When my ship is home again.

It's loaded down with sunshine
  Enough to go around,
In my beautiful dream ship
  Now homeward bound.
It carries all good wishes
  And love for everyone,
Happiness of every kind
  And loads and loads of fun.

Come down to the landing
  Where you can also greet,
My wonderful, wonderful dream ship
  Sailing the sea so deep.
Don't worry if you've quarrelled
  With your sweetheart dear,
For there's a balm for that too
  That will bring good cheer.

For you, who feel hopeless
  Think the world is cold,
Your heart I'll fill with warmth and love
  More precious even than gold.
If you have lost some loved one
  A father or mother dear,
You must not grieve about them
  You must dry every tear.

That is why this dream ship
  Is sailing o'er the sea,
Just to bring loads of sunshine
  To folks like you and me.
You'll know it by its beauty
  Colorful as the sky,
With reflections of the rainbow
  Telling you joy is nigh.

I hope that it will be here soon
  For I saw it in my dreams,
When the moon was high in the heavens
  Casting its silvery beams.
So let each one come smiling
  And you shall go with me,
To meet my treasured dream ship
  That's sailing o'er the sea.

[20]

DREAMY BLUE EYES

I often wonder where you are,
　My dreamy, blue eyed girl;
Your lips are like a rose bud,
　Each tooth a shining pearl.
The nights, so long and dreary,
　Make me sad and blue;
I am longing for you, darling;
　My love is just for you.

Forgive me, oh, forgive me!
　Don't be angry, dear;
I'm sorry, oh, so sorry;
　I've lost your love, I fear.
Be sweet to me, my blue eyed girl;
　There's something I would say;
I want you and I need you,
　So won't you name the day?

Come back to me, forget the past.
　I'll hold you in my arms;
I'll let the love that burns within
　Shield you from all alarms.
Beneath the moon, so clear and bright,
　I'll wait alone for you.
Come back, my dreamy, blue eyed girl,
　You'll find my heart is true.

THE COMING OF OLD AGE

When your steps begin to falter
　And your eyes are growing dim,
When your hair is all so silvery
　And you tremble in each limb,
You will wonder what has caused this
　And you'll think you'd best look out,
But that's old age creeping on you
　Your mind need have no doubt.

When music loses all its charm
　And you no longer want to dance,
Or make love to every charmer
　When you get the chance,
When you get no thrill in holding hands.
　As in days of long ago,
That is old age creeping on you
　Bending down your head so low.

So now's the time to step aside
　Let youth take your place,
Boys you know must have their fling
　And you have run your race,
Time is restless, will not wait
　And is turning o'er the page,
Take your place beside the fire
　Accept the coming of old age.

[21]

GARDEN OF MEMORIES

MY SUNSHINE

There is one whom I long to see,
And with whom I long to be,
She is the one I shall always love,
My Angel whose destiny is above.

There is one whom I long to greet,
And Oh, the joy when we shall meet,
To me she is the only girl,
My sweetheart, wife, and precious pearl.

When in darkness and gloom,
Her letters my nature did bloom,
Because when I read each line,
I knew things went well with My Sunshine.

A TRIBUTE TO MOTHER

This day we pay our tribute
To the greatest woman of all,
Who loved us from our infancy,
Is always at our call;
Who never was too tired
To listen to our woes,
Stood ready to protect us
From the world's cruel blows.

There's no love like a mother's love;
Though you fall, she'll love you still;
Though condemned by the whole wide world,
She'll cling to you through every ill.
No matter what has been your lot,
Or what conditions have brought about,
You are to her the same sweet child;
In her heart you'll find no doubt.

Those who have their mother, dear,
Should do all within their power,
To love and to protect her,
That her life be a golden hour.
But we who have no mother,
Save in the silent grave,
Are denied her tender care,
And love that makes one brave.

When our hearts are crushed with sorrow,
If mother were only here,
We could go to her for guidance,
Rest under her protecting care.
Gentle mother, we would thank you
For training us in our youth,
For all your loving kindness,
And showing us the truth.

[22]

WHEN MANDY CAME SNEAKING HOME

Early this morning, about four o'clock,
  Mandy came home, Mandy came home;
But when she got there the door was locked,
  When Mandy came home, when Mandy came home.
She cried, "Oh, Daddy, won't you open that door?
  I'll not stay out late any more.
But I slept right on, as I did before
  Mandy came sneaking home.

I turned right over in my good soft bed,
  When Mandy came home, when Mandy came home;
I tucked the pillows high under my head,
  When Mandy came home, when Mandy came home.
She said, "Oh, Daddy don't be mean to me,
  I'm just as sorry as I can be."
I went on snoring right merrily
  When Mandy came lagging home.

She made so much noise I had to open the door,
  When Mandy came home, when Mandy came home,
And by this time I was good and sore,
  When Mandy came home, when Mandy came home.
I said to her: "Now, look here, gal,
I've found someone else to be my pal.
You can do the same, or live alone."
                              (This line to be spoken)
That's what I said,
  When Mandy came sneaking home.

A MESSAGE FROM A ROSE

I found this little rose bud
  Withering in the street
It had not lost it's color
  To me it looked so sweet.
I took it and caressed it
  And pressed it to my heart
As each petal whispered
  How can we ever part.

And it is this little rosebud
  I am sending now to you
Listen to it's story
  Each word so fond and true.
Though distance lies between us
  My heart for you so yearns,
My love is just as steadfast
  And the fire of hope still burns.

[23]

[207]

WHEN I GET OVER THERE

My soul will find expression
  When I get over there;
I'll feel no sad depression
  When I get over there;
Where the saints play harps and sing
Glorious praises to Christ our king,
And the Heavens with music ring—
  When I get over there.

My robe will be all snowy white
  When I get over there;
My soul will reach its utmost height
  When I get over there.
Christ will take me by the hand
And show me through the Promised Land;
All the world's sufferings I'll understand,
  When I get over there.

MY DEAR OLD HONEY MOON

I am waiting, Honey Moon,
  And watching for your light;
So shed your silvery radiance
  To make my pathway bright.
There's someone waiting to greet me
  Down by the old saw mill;
She's the only girl I've ever loved,
  And I know she loves me still.

So shine out, Honey Moon,
  I've something I would tell,
But I need your mystic presence
  To help me weave the spell.
I'd tell it to the nightingale
  Whose notes are weird and low;
I'd tell it to the twinkling stars
  And rushing winds that blow.

So shine out, Honey Moon;
  Don't withhold your light;——
When the purple clouds roll back
  This enchanted night.
I see the stars a twinkling,
  And there shines my Honey Moon.
Stay out until I tell her all—
  But don't peep while we spoon.

[24]

GUARDIAN ANGEL

Beneath the willow trees
   Lies my mother dear;
No one can fill the space,
   She left vacant here.
Her smile, so inspiring,
   Would assure and .cheer;
She was an angel here on earth
   My own mother dear.

I was just a little tot
   When she pressed me to her heart;
And told me God had called her
   And soon we'd have to part.
Oh, how I have missed
   Her kind and loving care;
This world has never been the same
   Since she went over there.

When her spirit soared away
   To the realms of bliss;
To me she said a sweet goodbye
   With a lingering kiss.
Some day I'll surely meet her
   Where the angels stand;
In the midst of glory
   In the Promised Land.

So these lines mother dear
   I now dedicate to you;
In fond rememberance
   Of you, so fine, so true
When I lay me down to sleep,
   I softly shed a tear
For you, my Guardian Angel,
   For you, my mother dear.

HOME

In the silence of the night,
   I sit all alone;
Alone by the fireside,
   Thinking of home;
Mother and Dad,
   Their faces must beam,
As they see me drifting,
   Home in my dream.

I think of my childhood,
   And the place of my birth,
Oh, there's no place
   Like the family hearth.
I'll never forget them,
   As I drift down life's stream,
Mother and Dad,
   And the home of my dreams.

PICTURES AT TWILIGHT

The summer clouds at twilight,
    Are drifting, drifting low,
And their purple shadows,
    Hide the moonlight's glow;
But soon its mirrored beauty,
    Will shine out clear and bright
And shed upon our pathway,
    Its soft and mystic light.

When the clouds at twilight,
    Go drifting, drifting by,
You'll see what God has painted,
    On his easel in the sky;
And in the hush of eventide,
    Sweet memories you will share,
In all the pristine beauty,
    You'll find painted there.

MOTHER ALWAYS UNDERSTANDS

A Mother's love is the truest love
    No matter what may betide,
Should trouble cross your pathway,
    She'll hasten to your side,
With heart full of tenderness,
    She'll take you by the hands,
Kiss the worries from your brow,
    For Mother always understands.

She recalls your childhood days,
    When things would go amiss,
If by chance you hurt yourself,
    She'd heal it with a kiss.
If you go to her in grief,
    She'd meet you with healing hands,
She'll shield you with all her love,
    For Mother always understands.

As you journey down life's pathway,
    And if you find it smooth,
Then you should help your mother too,
    And all her heartaches try and soothe,
If you've been blessed with riches,
    And you have a home so grand,
Share them all with her dear,
    Let her know you understand.

When her steps begin to falter,
    And her hair is turning gray,
Love her, and remember this,
    She will so soon pass away;
When she joins the angelic host
    She'll guide you with unseen hands,
She'll watch over you from Heaven,
    For Mother always understands.

[26]

MY SOUTHERN HOME

I long for old Mississippi,
My dear Southern home,
To see fields of cotton blossom
As o'er the hills I'd roam,
To where the birds sing sweetest,
Midst the tall sugar cane,
I long for my home in the Southland,
I yearn to see it again.

I'd sit there in the moonlight,
When the stars were all aglow,
Listening to sweetest harmony,
From banjoes, soft and low,
To hear the boat's shrill whistle,
Would be music to my ear,
In my home in the dear old Southland
The place I love so dear.

Chorus

Down the Mississippi let's go sailing,
Sailing to that sunny, sunny clime,
To tho land that is the dearest,
Where life would be sublime;
We'd harmonize in the evening,
And drive dull cares away,
Let's go sailing down the Mississippi,
Sailing with hearts so gay.

THE SHADOWY LONG AGO

My soul is sick within me
For the hours away from you;
Anxious and lonely, waiting,
Discouraged through and through.
My brain seems clogged and weary,
My hands refuse to work,
My feet drag slow beneath me,
My hands their duty shirk.

When the day fades into twilight,
And darkening shadows fall,
That is when I am loneliest
And miss you most of all.
I should let by-gones be by-gones;
'Twould not be human, though.
Our minds will still drift backward
To the shadowy long ago.

THE SOUL OF AN ARTIST

The soul of an artist
   Is akin to the rose;
Crudeness, unkindness,
   Disturbs its repose.

It's in tune with the infinite,
   And lives on a plane,
Where thoughts are all golden,
   And true love's not vain.

This soul is so beautiful,
   Sensitive and true,
Of exquisite delicacy,
   Pure as the dew.

When sorrow and disaster
   Blast such a soul,
It will wither and fade,
   And death take it's toll.

THE SPIRIT OF LOVE

I am the Spirit of Love,
   I travel everywhere;
I visit the hovels
   And homes of loving care.
I am the Spirit of Love,
   Am a link in the chain;
I help bear your sorrows
   And I soothe your pain.

Without the Spirit of Love
   Life will be of no avail;
Without the Spirit of Love
   Your efforts will but fail.
I make the stars shine brighter,
   I drive grief away;
I bring smiles to faces
   That reflect Love's loving way.

So I, the Spirit of Love,
   Am sending out today,
Wireless messages,
   Thru the Milky Way.
The mind, the absorbing station,
   Is abundantly supplied,
With the Spirit of Love,
   But must be tenderly applied.

GOD'S GIFT TO MANKIND

God sends to us the sunshine
  As well as the gentle rain,
The skies that are so beautiful
  And also the golden grain;
Tho grass so like the emerald
  Tho winds that whisper low,
The stars and tho moon to shine at night
  After the sunset's glow.

The birds to cheer us on our way
  As they sing from the treetops green,
The little pool with laughing rills,
  And the forest, a verdant scene;
Tho whipporwill with its sad notes
  And tho nightingale's wistful tune,
The perfume of the clover field,
  And tho mystic nights of June.

God said there must be darkness
  And His word a law became;
He also sent the beautiful dawn
  And tho lightning like a flame;
He said there would be happiness
  And joys for us untold,
If we kept to the path of righteousness
  His love He would unfold.

So we're thankful for the sunshine
  And for his wondrous love,
And for His forgiving powers
  And the glowing stars above;
All we see that is beautiful
  Was sent from Him to man,
To reveal to him in the smallest way
  A part of His heavenly plan.

THE STORM

I heard the wind howling,
  I shuddered with dread;
As it moaned and it groaned,
  As though tears it would shed.
I drew the shades lower
  To shut out the night;
I sat in a tremor,
  I quivered with fright.

It kept up its shrieking,
  It drove me almost mad,
I wrung my hands wildly,
  I felt lost and sad.
Then my eyes slowly opened,
  I found it a dream,
I'll always remember
  When wild night winds scream.

THE VISION

A sacred rose bush
  Grew in a monastery;
Many years, years ago;
  They called it St. Mary.
The monks would worship beside it,
  And if their prayers were heard,
A vision of Mary appeared,
  Her veil by the winds bestirred.

With her hand on the bush,
  Roses bloomed mysteriously,
In clusters of threes,
  Representing the Trinity.
A girl overheard this story,
  And said she'd do the same;
She would pose beside the rose bush,
  And bring her lover fame.

They stole into the sacred walls,
  She beautiful and fair;
He placed her hand on the bush,
  And draped a veil o'er her hair.
As her hand touched the rose bush,
  Her expression quickly changed;
The artist painted madly,
  Lest her pose become disarranged.

During the recreation hour,
  One monk saw her through the leaves.
He raised his eyes to Heaven,
  As he fell upon his knees.
He lay upon the sward,
  And was found there by the rest.
He told them of what he'd seen,
  And at last he had been blest.

The rose bush had bloomed,
  And the Madonna's face he'd seen;
Her eyes were raised to Heaven,
  O'erhead a golden sheen.
She felt that she had done a wrong,
  And vowed the truth she'd tell;
Her lover begged and pleaded,
  But her conscience she could not quell.

She was a changed girl 'tis said,
  As she walked through the grounds once more.
To confer with the Father,
  And tell him her past was o'er.
He told her that in every woman
  There is sacredness to be found;
While her hand was on the bush
  Holiness was shown profound.
She made a vow to Heaven,
  To follow where the Saints had trod;
And would never look backward,
  But would ever serve her God.

[30]

MY HOME IN VIRGINIA

My heart yearns for old Virginia,
    The place where I was born;
Where the song-birds sweetly warble,
    In the fields of sugar corn.
It is there that I am going,
    To calm my dear mother's fears,
To feel her tender arms around me,
    And see her welcoming tears.

At night, when stars are shining,
    And the moon peeps o'er the ridge,
I'll walk a well-known pathway,
    Across the swinging bridge;
There I'll view my home surroundings,
    As I wait for my sweetheart;
She'll meet me in the twilight,
    And we shall never part.

We'll walk where the moon shines brightest,
    Where the sweet magnolias grow,
To our old rose-covered cottage,
    As the whispering breezes blow.
Then my mother dear will bless me,
    And I'll kiss her smiling face,
And I'll stay in old Virginia;
    Oh, how I long for that dear place.

IF I WERE A BOY

If you were only me, my dear,
    And I were just, say, you,
I would change things a bit—
    I'll tell you what I'd do.

I'd send a box of candy
    Or sweetmeats of some kind,
And maybe a bunch of violets—
    Then my love you'd not decline.

And then, again, I'd telephone,
    And ask to take you out,
Not leave you in solitude,
    Your mind filled with doubt.

I'd take you to see a movie;
    It need not be of great renown;
As long as we were together,
    Our joy would be profound.

I would try to make you happy
    If I were a boy like you;
And I wouldn't mind saying, either,
    That I loved you too.

[31]

MOTHER'S LOVE

A Mother's love is true and tried
And deeper than the ocean wide
She watches over you with tenderest care
Shield's your path from every snare.
She thinks of you all thru the day
Whether you are near or far away
And tho' you are loved by sisters and brothers
You'll find their love is not like mother's.

Her thoughts of you are always pure
And of her love you're always sure
She toiled for you with but a sigh
She's happiest when you are nigh.
And as she greets you with her kiss
She knows when things have gone amiss
And tho you're loved by many others
You'll find this love is not like mother's.

When mother's life slowly ebbs away
She prays that you'll not be led astray
From the straight and narrow path
Thus bringing on your head God's wrath.
When at last she's claimed by death
Leaving you sad and much bereft
Her spirit will come back thru the deep
To watch and assure you peaceful sleep.

———

HEART PANGS

I did not mean to hurt you,
Or cause the tears to fall,
My desire was to please you,
As I loved you best of all;
But you left the one who loves you,
Who longed for your caresses,
Yearned to hear of your love,
As you smoothed my tresses.

But weary hours and days passed,
No word came from you,
I drooped with the twilight,
So lonesome and so blue;
My heart with anguish breaking,
Because of love profound,
Pangs pierced like needles,
My sorrows knew no bounds.

At night there came a specter,
A ghost into my life had crept,
In my waking hours it vanished,
But hovered o'er me while I slept;
But I have since been taught,
How to smile again,
I am now protected by one,
Who will sooth away my pain.

[32]

WINTER

THE BEAUTIFUL SNOW FLAKES

The snow flakes are scurrying over the hills,
Stinging our faces and giving us thrills;
Rolling and tossing, tumbling with glee,
Dashing and flashing, so merrily;
Pure as the lily they fall from the sky,
Flake after flake goes swiftly by;
A whirlwind of beauty they eddy along,
As rhythmically as a sweet Christmas song.

Soft as a feather they fall from the sky,
With crystal like beauty they sail swiftly by;
Whirling and twirling they dash along
Kissing the faces of the happy throng
Now see the snow birds with great delight
Hopping about on this carpet of white;
Then flying to the bushes and trees;
They don't seem to mind the cold Winter breeze.

SPRING TIME

Be happy in the sunshine,
  Be happy in the rain,
Be happy as a mocking bird,
  For spring is here again.
Just forget your sorrows,
  Throw aside all care,
For the zephyr breezes are blowing,
  The trees no longer bare.

Go out in the wildwood,
  With nature be in tune,
The ferns are so dainty,
  And the violets are in bloom.
The little daffodils you'll find,
  In sweet simplicity,
You'll also find the humming birds,
  And the busy little bee.

Clover heads peeping,
  From the mossy dell,
And you'll find columbine,
  And the daisies that never tell.
Birds sweetly singing,
  From tree tops green,
And the dense hedges,
  For nature's romantic screen.

And over on the hillside,
  Runs the little babbling brook,
And you'll find, beyond, the shepherd
  Guiding his sheep with a crook.
And many other wonders,
  If you'll only seek to find,
You'll then forget all sorrow,
  And leave the world behind.

[33]

THE CHRISTMAS TREE

Over the mountains high
  Snowy and white
Come's dear old Santa Clause
  Every Christmas eve night.
His reindeer are swift,
  They glisten with ice
His sleigh, it is laden
  With everything nice.

He lights on the house top
  Down the chimney he'll peep
To see if the children
  Are all fast asleep.
Then he'll slide softly down
  More quiet than a mouse,
Hang up the stocking
  Then slip from the house.

So with sleigh bells ringing
  His eyes dancing with glee,
He'll pick out the presents
  For the next Christmas Tree.
He wishes much happiness
  For the girls and the boys
He's quite sure they'll have fun
  With their new Christmas toys.

There are skates and a wagon
  For Willie and Joe,
A doll and a buggy
  For Lula and Flo.
Father some handkerchiefs
  With dotes in the corner,
Bob a story book
  About Jack Horner.

Mother and Granny
  Are as happy as we
For they too have presents
  On our Christmas Tree.

CHRISTMAS CHIMES

Christmas Chimes, Christmas Chimes,
Ring out! Ring out once more!
With harps and many voices,
A Savior to adore;
The born in lowly manger,
And of such humble birth,
He is now the King of Glory,
Let gladness fill the earth.

Christmas Chimes, Christmas Chimes,
Ring out our Christmas song,
As we sing of a Savior's love
Blend with the earthly throng;
Jesus came from Heaven,
To die that we might live,
And of His wondrous bounty,
To all He'll freely give.

Christmas Chimes, Christmas Chimes,
May you reach the heathen land,
And spread the joyful tidings,
That all may understand;
Christmas Chimes, Christmas Chimes,
Ring. and ring, and ring!
So Jesus Christ in glory,
Will listen while we sing.

THE SUNSET HOUR

It was the hour of sunset,
The sky was all aglow;
The sun in its majesty
Was casting rays below.
This crimson ball of beauty
Enthralled me by its power—
The rarest sight I've ever seen,
The sunset hour.

It looked as though 'twere blushing
Against the sky of blue,
In its artistic setting
'Midst clouds of purple hue.
Unmindful of the perfume
Wafted from the bower,
I stood in awe of the beauty
Of the sunset hour.

Slowly then it hid from view
Behind a shifting cloud,
And soon the darkening shadows fell,
Enveloping meek and proud.
Could I but blend the coloring,
As I sit in my rose hued bower,
I'd paint a picture immortal
Of God's own sunset hour.

[35]

[219]

THE CALL OF THE FOREST

If I had the wings of a bird
  I would soar far far away
Over the tops of the verdant hills
  To satisfy my heart's desire
That deep within me is stirred

I would fly over the mountain green
  And come down in mossy dells
When the sun sank in the golden west
  I would seek shelter and sweet rest
With forest of trees for my screen.

And when the mist cleared away
  And the morning dawned rosy and bright
I would take flight and soar up high
  To view the beautiful rainbow sky
And admire it's beauty by day.

I would drink of limpid streams
  To quench my throat of it's thirst
When the sun gave way for wind and showers,
  I would seek shelter in moss covered bowers
Away from the world that's not what it seems.

MY SILVERY MOON

Oh moon, my silvery moon
  With your beauty, so fair, so bright
The world would be in darkness
  If it were not for you and your light
You go over the mountains bleak
  And over verdant hills
You come down thru lowly valleys
  And reflect in the laughing rills.

You penetrate the darkness
  And like the morning star
You guide the weary traveler
  Who journeys from afar.
And when the Snow King's with us
  And the world is glistening white
Your silvery light that gives a touch
  That brings to all delight.

The nights would be so dreary
  If it were not for you
Though the stars do twinkle lightly
  And the sky is always blue.
They do not lend enchantment
  They do not glorify
As you do with your light so bright
  Sailing softly by.

[36]

LET'S GLORIFY HIM

On His Throne in the Kingdom,
  Sits our Savior so dear;
He was nailed to the Cross,
  And died without fear.
He came meek and lowly,
  To cleanse us from sin;
To give Life Eternal,
  Let's Glorify Him.

There'll come a bright radiance,
  That will light up the sky;
While we bow at the altar,
  And Angels draw nigh.
Some day in His presence
  We'll reverently sing,
"Exalt Him! Exalt Him!"
  And laud Him, Our King.

Many years may roll by,
  Before Gabriel will stand,
And sound his great Trumpet,
  For the vast Holy Band,
To descend to the Faithful,
  With their wings of love,
To ascend to Jesus,
  To their Home above.

He's Risen! He's Risen!
  He Conquered the grave.
Exalt Him! Exalt Him!
  Our Savior so brave.
So this Easter morning,
  Let's thankfully sing,
And Glorify Jesus,
  Our Crucified King.

CHRIST THE LORD IS RISEN

Christ is risen, Christ is risen,
  Christ is risen from the dead;
On the cruel cross He suffered,
  On Calvary's mount His blood was shed.
Just to save us, just to save us,
  Just to save our souls from sin,
They nailed our Savior to the cross—
  Oh, the agonizing pain within!

Christ is risen, Christ is risen,
  Now He reigns in Heaven above;
But he redeemed us, he redeemed us
  With his everlasting love.
Let us praise Him, let us praise Him,
  God the Father, and the Holy Ghost.
It was they who raised Him from the dead
  That we might join the heavenly host.

| 37 |

JESUS IS MINE

Oh my Heavenly Savior I've found
  Jesus is mine,
He's always the same His love is profound
  His blessing divine.
He's waiting and listening thru all the day
As I watch sincerely and pray
For He is the truth the light and the way
  Jesus is mine

Oh, what a comfort He is to me,
  Jesus, mine,
His blood was shed to set me free
  His love divine.
He led me from darkness into light
And now my soul is shining bright.
You don't know how happy I am tonight
  For Jesus is mine.

I have drunk from the Fountain of life,
  Jesus is mine,
I shall cease from all my earthly strife
  And let my light shine
Into the world filled with greed
  I shall sow spirtual seed
Now His love fills every need
  Jesus is mine.

For the rest of my life He'll lead the way
  Jesus is mine
Lest my footsteps should falter and stray
  Oh hope divine.
Far away in Heaven some day
The Savior will wash my sins away
Then I will rejoice and proclaim and say
  Jesus is mine.

DAWN OF LOVE

The moon through shadows dark,
  Is skimming o'er the lake,
Two lovers in their little barque,
  Drift lazily on e'er morning breaks;
Their faces reflect their heart's content,
  As they gaze in each other's eyes,
Soul meets soul in fond embrace,
  As the moonlight slowly dies.

They had crossed the lake to the Village,
  Where the nuptial knot was tied,
He is now a happy bridegroom,
  And she a blushing bride.
May their lives be always happy,
  No matter what e'er betide,
May he always think of the girl he loves,
  As his beautiful charming bride.

[38]

ROSE PETALS

Rose Petals, Rose Petals, tell me please,
    The secret held deep in your pretty leaves;
You who are still as fragrantly sweet
    As when on the bush the morning you'd greet;
I know you were handled with tender care,
    Rose Petals, Rose Petals, once so fair.

Did they drink from your perfume expelled,
    And gasp in ecstasy when you they beheld
Glistening and scintillating with dew,
    Rose Petals, Rose Petals, tell me true
You flirted with lovers, that I know
    A Will O' the Wisp told me so.

You cast o'er them a magic spell
    To intoxicate—you knew full well.
Please tell me your secret, I'll come out tonight,
    When the moon is shedding its shafts of light.
I want to know how deep was the part
    You played on the strings of the human heart.

NOTE: *I was inspired to write this poem by looking
at crushed petals of roses once worn by
Madame Schuman Heink, whom I had the
pleasure of serving in my professional capacity.*
           MAZIE EARHART CLARK.

MY ROSE DREAM

There grew in my garden a beautiful rose,
    It reminded me, sweetheart, of you;
Its beauty and fragrance filled the air,
    As the summer winds gently blew.
It seemed to weave a charm for me,
    And the rose it became your heart,
And then your form I could faintly see
    As of the bush it became a part.

All roses are beautiful, that I know,
    But if I could have my pick,
I would choose the rose that's crimson,
    Although its thorns did prick.
You are the rose that blooms for me,
    You are the one whom I love.
Oh, come with me to my Garden of Dreams,
    Where the stars shine brightly above.

For in the distance I hear a bell,
    In the church where the red ramblers grow,
And the tendrills of two hearts become entwined—
    That's the place where they should go.
I will make you so happy, my sweetheart,
    For me you shall bloom alone;
My heart shall be your Garden of Love,
    And without you it's as heavy as stone.

THE CIRCUS

The morning dawned clear and bright,
  And the sun sent a golden ray
Over the throng of eager faces
  Waiting for the parade so gay.
First came the mounted officers.
  To clear the right of way.
In the distance the band was playing,
  And the crowd began to sway.

The acrobats on their handsome steeds,
  Smiled as they passed along;
The clowns with their grimaces
  There singing a tuneless song.
One played upon his cornet
  With a dull stare on his face,
Then bowed from side to side
  With a clown's clumsy grace.

The animals also played their parts,
  Elephants and wild cats, too;
There were vendors of peanuts and lemonade,
  And bootleggers selling home brew.
Then as usually happens
  When a circus comes to town—
The sun hid itself behind a cloud,
  And the rain came pouring down.

THE GRUMBLER

There are folks who're always grumbling,
  Nothing seems just right,
And if you stopped to listen
  To their sad and lonely plight,
They'd talk about their neighbor,
  And their Preacher man,
They never seem quite able
  To fit into any plan.

If pork you'd have for dinner
  They'd ask you for a steak,
If you gave them plum pudding,
  They'd be sure to ask for cake.
If the fire was burning bright
  It was sure to be too hot,
Such folks are never satisfied,
  With whatever be their lot.

I wonder when they leave here,
  For the land of perfect bliss,
Will they find happiness over there
  Or will things still go amiss.
But that is life personified
  Reaching for the stars,
They never will be satisfied
  Tho' transported to the Land of Mars.

SPIRITUAL BIRTH

We go to bed, then we arise,
  Hoping each day for some new surprise,
But the world goes on in the same old way,
  Dusk fades into night, then comes the day;
To enjoy the dawn with perfect delight,
  Our minds must be quite clear and bright,
We'll then get the best the world affords,
  Smiles, Sunshine and Cheery Words.

Let us climb to the utmost height,
  Let our souls find harmony and light,
Let us develop as we comprehend,
  And with the Great Spirit blend;
And as we go on hand in hand,
  Striving to reach the Promised Land,
That can only be reached thru faith and love,
  And earned passport to Heaven above.

To reach that mansion not built with hands,
  Where life is perpetual and never ends,
Day after day we must grow in grace,
  To enable us to enter that holy place.
We must first know a Spiritual Birth,
  E're God's angels carry us from earth,
To sing and worship at Jesus' feet,
  Where our happiness will be complete.

THE UNSOLVED MYSTERY

I wonder what great mysteries
  Await us over there,
A place we hear so much about,
  But which we seem to fear,
It's a place of pure delight,
  Where love must ever reign.
There can be no sorrows there,
  And we will never know pain.

In the land that awaits us,
  We all have a place to fill,
Over there we'll be with Jesus,
  Doing His Holy Will.
Our hearts will be so happy,
  For they'll be free from sin,
And where there once was darkness
  A light will glow within.

We'll be one of the host,
  As we'll leave the earth some day,
But we must follow the steps of Jesus
  Watch, as well as pray.
Then when the call does come to us,
  And all mysteries are revealed,
We'll understand, dear Jesus,
  And why he kept them concealed.

[41]

MEMORIES' HALL

I hear sweet strains of music,
  Playing soft and low,
It makes my heart turn backward,
  To the long, long ago;
I held you in my arms dear,
  Its thrills I still recall,
When we danced just you and I,
  Around memories' hall.

You told me that you loved me,
  And you'd be mine some day,
I said that I'd be true to you,
  My love would never stray;
I long to have you near me,
  You're the dearest girl of all,
Come let us waltz just you and I,
  Around Memories' Hall.

Chorus
We'll sway with the music,
  As I look into your eyes,
You'll cling to me so tenderly,
  As the moonlight slowly dies;
When stars twinkle dimly,
  We'll say goodnight to all,
Once more we'll waltz Home Sweet Home,
  Around Memories' Hall.

THE LOVERS

Dusk has fallen o'er the land,
  The stars are twinkling bright,
The lake looms up serenely,
  Shimmering thru the night;
The moonbeams glimmer thru the trees,
  Where nymphs are wont to roam,
Waiting to crown the lovers' heads,
  As they dance before their throne.

It is the hour for making love,
  All nature is in tune,
When sweethearts leave the world behind,
  In the arms of night to sweetly swoon;
And there renew their vows of love,
  With many a sigh and kiss,
Promising to be ever true,
  Visioning a future of perfect bliss.

[42]

MY OWN DEAR VALENTINE

Did you ever treasure,
　Just a simple valentine,
With a Cupid's bow and arrow,
　And a loving rhyme,
'Till it had grown yellow,
　From the years that had gone by?
You remember when it came,
　You breathed a happy sigh.

Did you fondle it,
　And fancy he was near,
And could almost hear him say
　"How I love you dear"?
There's a secret I shall tell you,
　But I must whisper soft and low,
I have such a Valentine,
　With a Cupid and a bow.

The archer came and got him,
　He went, I know not where,
I see him in dreamland,
　With his friend Robin Adair.

So I am sending out this message,
　To the land of sunshine,
So he'll know that I am waiting,
　For my own dear Valentine.

A TRUE FRIEND

The kind of friend of whom you'd boast,
　Is not the one smilingly giving a toast,
He may be just a fairweather friend,
　On such my dear, you could not depend.
Should you find one true and tried,
　Who'd stick to you at the turn of the tide,
When you are left to stand alone
　With a smile on his face he'd take you home.

Where you'd be as welcome as a day in Spring,
　Joy and happiness to you he'd bring,
He'll study your welfare and see that you hear,
　Only the things that your heart holds dear,
And of his store he unselfishly gives,
　To go on thus as long as he lives.
If you should find such a good kind friend,
　Stick to him always, to whatever end.

[43]

GARDEN OF MEMORIES

WAITING FOR A LOVED ONE

I have lived long, but not in vain,
   And tho my place is filled when I am laid
In some shady spot where birds sweetly sing,
   Whereever my spirit goes, to you I'll cling;
I shall protect you, and with loving care,
   Guide your footsteps from every snare,
Sooth you when the world turns its back,
Be with you when true friends you lack.
Be with you in sickness or health,
Be with you if you should lose your wealth;
   Be with you in rain or in sunshine,
Be with you always because I am thine,
   And tho you see me on earth no more
I shall be waiting on the celestial shore,
   Waiting and watching just for you,
Because my love for you was true.

DEAR OLD DAD

No one knows how much we miss you,
   From the home you loved so dear,
When walking thru the garden,
   I cannot help but drop a tear
For the Dad who was so honest,
   Upright, faithful, kind and true,
Who loved us with deep sincerity,
   How can we help missing you?

Your chair at the table is still vacant,
   And the one you sat in beside the fire,
As you chatted with us at eventide,
   How your dear presence did inspire.
The life you lived while on earth,
   We are trying hard to emulate,
So when we're called up higher,
   We'll meet you at Heaven's pearly gate.
                His Daughter—Mazie.

THE OLD SCHOOLHOUSE

Dedicated to my teacher—Miss Lizzie Lawrence.

I wandered down a country lane,
To live o'er the long ago;
Down to the village schoolhouse,
When the sun was sinking low;
The pond we used to skate on,
Was dry, and in its stead,
Lay a park so beautiful,
Bedecked with roses red.

I stood upon the same old bank,
Where we watched the others skate,
It caused us many tear-drops,
Because of being late;
The teacher she would scold,
And keep us after school,
Some would get the rattan,
Others graced the dunce's stool.

Could I but call them back again,
The days of my childhood,
I would go to a secret nook,
Into the dense wildwood;
There I'd hold a conclave,
With the fairies in the dell,
I'd live o'er all the mysteries,
That held me in their spell.

As I stood lonely, dreaming,
Of days of long ago,
I heard voices singing,
The song, "Sweet and Low";
It came from the schoolhouse,
At the end of the lane.
Where others fill the places,
We'll n'er see again.

The weeping willows gave a sigh,
As I turned to wend my way,
From the dear old schoolhouse,
Where once I used to play;
I took with me fond memories,
Locked within my heart,
To remain there forever.
From them I'll never part.

[45]

BEAUTIFUL MOONBEAMS

I am in love with the beautiful moon,
Because it never tells when you spoon,
But casts over all a silvery ray
And peeps through the trees at hearts so gay.
Those who sit lonesome and sad,
It tries its best to make them glad
By shedding o'er them a flood of light,
Making their pathway ever bright.

I love to sit alone and gaze
At the moon and around it the misty haze;
It looks to me as though it smiles,
As it throws its radiance miles and miles.
Sprays of silver shoot through the leaves,
And the earth is fanned with a gentle breeze.
The enchantment of the perfumed night air
Brings joy to faces happy and fair.

Beautiful moon, I worship with you
The beautiful world and skies of blue.
When I awake from my slumber at night
You've bathed my chamber with silvery light.
I look through the window at you from afar,
And wonder, dear moon, just who you are.
You can't have a wife, for you stay out all night,
And keep your face radiantly bright.

So you must be a bachelor, my dear Mr. Moon;
That's the reason the girls hate going in too soon.
You lend enchantment to the garden of roses,
And exasperation to the boy who proposes;
And the maid you charm when she looks at you,
And whispers to her lover, "Yes, I'll be true;"
And when you leave and go under a cloud
The earth is wrapped in night's dark shroud.

The birds tuck their heads more snugly in their nest
Under the protection of the mother bird's breast;
And all nature seems to have gone fast asleep,
And here and there a few twinkling stars peep;
And I too once more go back to my bed,
And before I know it the night has fled.
I have all day to think of my dear Mr. Moon,
And tonight I will not go to bed so soon.

THE BEST THINGS IN LIFE

We are born in this world of trouble and strife,
    Yet we are unwilling to give up life;
We struggle with problems we're burdened with care,
    And of happiness we have our share.
We stop to figure what it's all about,
    But when we've finished we've found nothing out;
We leave baby days, and soon mature,
    To man and womanhood—that is Nature.

Well, now that we've reached the dangerous age,
    Day after day when we turn a new page,
Do not falter, be sturdy and true,
    Give to the world, that is watching you,
Something to think of when you are gone,
    And always be ready to help along;
Be a tower of strength to the men you meet,
    It costs nothing to kindly greet.

You may meet someone with a broken heart,
    Or someone who has made the wrong start;
A word kindly spoken, or just a smile,
    Will cheer one for a long, long while;
And when we do the things that are right,
    We'll go around with a countenance bright;
'Twill relieve the sadness of one's heart,
    When we unselfishly do our part.

Matters not the color or the creed,
    Be a power of powers, sowing good seed,
Life is precious, so have a care,
    In all our dealings let us be fair;
Be not deceitful, be open and frank,
    And not wound others with silly pranks;
And be not the cause of someone going astray,
    If you are guilty you'd better pray.

We are passing this way only once,
    So let us not play the part of a dunce,
For deeds of kindness will blaze the trail,
    When in darkness we've left the vale,
When we have crossed the Great Divide,
We'll meet the only One we cannot deride,
So let us, while in this world of strife,
    Check up and do the BEST THINGS IN LIFE.

ON CALVARY'S BROW

I know that Jesus suffered agony for me;
I know that on Calvary He died to set me free;
Still I am not brave enough to stand before the crowd
And there exalt His holy name, With head lowly bowed.

But from deep within my sinful heart
My soul does rise in prayer;
And Jesus knows the turmoil there,
For he is everywhere.
Jesus Jesus Give me strength,
Comfort me with thy power;
Guide my faltering footsteps
In this, my anxious hour.

The time is coming all too soon,
When I'll meet him face to face
And stand before his majestic throne,
A sinner saved by grace.
I pray thee now, dear Jesus,
Do make me meek and mild;
Make me pure within
As an innocent little child.

Help me observe the Golden Rule
And treat my neighbor fair,
And with the poor within my gates
My earthly riches share.
I want the Divine Spirit
To purge my soul of sin,
So my crucified Savior
Will come and enter in.

Then in the shadow of death
I shall have no fear,
Although there may be demons
Lurking everywhere.
I'll remember thy cheering words
Fear not, I am the way,
The truth and the light
That shines in the world to day.

Then I shall lay my weary head,
Upon your gentle breast;
Then while you fold me in your arms,
I'll sink to my peaceful rest.

[48]

"LINDY"

(America's Boy)

Up through the clouds
  Flew an auto of the breeze,
Over fields and meadows
  And stately old trees;
Sped a lone rider
  As on wings of a dove,
As sure of his flight
  As of the stars above.

Alone drove Lindy,
  O'er mountains and hills;
Watching the switchboard
  Gave him great thrills.
He pulled back the lever
  And soared in mid-air.
It was a brave feat
  That but few would dare.

He thought of his mother
  And her smiling face,
Of her noble teachings
  And her gentle grace.
"Charles," said the mother,
  "I know that you'll win;
My prayers will go with you
  As lightly you spin".

The news was flashed back
  That he had crossed the sea,
As all eyes were watching
  For him in Paree.
God was his pilot,
  With his all-seeing eyes,
Led him to victory
  Through sleet-laden skies.

Lindy has always been
  His mother's joy,
But we claim him now
  As America's boy.
Unspoiled by the honors
  On land and on sea,
May history record
  The name—"L-I-N-D-Y."

BABY'S KISSES

The wicked ones still roam the earth
  Who fostered the cruel deed,
Seared two loving, trusting hearts,
  To satisfy their worldly greed;
Poor innocent little baby,
  Taken from his home,
While wrapped in the arms of Morpheus,
  Unprotected and all alone.

Dreaming dreams, perhaps of angels,
  With a smile on his face so dear,
Or he may have just awakened,
  Sensing the danger drawing near.
Where is Daddy? Where is Mother?
  Must have been his frightened thoughts,
As they crushed him, the little darling,
  Oh what sorrow thus was wrought.

They have closed the secret chamber,
  That for him is set apart,
There sweet memories will remain,
  In the depths of their sad hearts;
Thru the silence comes his spirit,
  In the quiet of the night,
Baby's kisses like the breezes,
  Will touch them with lips so light.

Baby arms will twine around them,
  He'll nestle close on Mother's breast,
He will sooth and caress them,
  While in dreamland they rest;
Day by day time passes onward,
  And in the twilight of your life,
May your clouds be rose and silver,
  May you escape worldly strife.

The whole world grieves with you, Lindy,
  And your little wife so dear,
Your sorrows were universal,
  And the world shed many a tear;
God loves and will protect you,
  But on Him you must believe,
He's the one who heals all sorrows,
  Of your burdens he will relieve.

THE HANDS OF FATE

Fate follows your steps
    Wherever you go
Tho' you make every effort
    Good seeds to sow.
You may strictly regard
    The old golden rule
You were taught when a child
    Going to school.

Fate, stalks after you
    From your birth to your grave
Tho' worries oppress you
    You try to be brave.
But what is the use
    You'll say after all
Like Adam and Eve
    Due for a fall.

Fate weaves her web
    Around two loving hearts
Brings them together
    Then them ruthlessly parts.
They could have been happy
    If just left alone
But fate stood waiting
    To wreck their home.

Fate seems so cruel
    Fate seems unfair
Fate breaks two hearts
    Drives them to despair.
It relentlessly grasps
    With the grip of steel
Until you give in
    To whatever fate wields.

Hope finally dies
    In each weary breast
Then we long for the place
    Where we can find rest.
Tho' the forces change
    It would be too late
The chain has been forged
    And welded by fate.

THE CALL OF AN IDNIAN MAID

The Indian maid sat at her loom
There she seemed to be busily weaving
   But her thoughts drifted far
   To brave Shooting Star
Who, alas, would soon be leaving.

Together they strolled by the brook
No care did she know 'til one day
   When a pale faced man
   From a distant land
Came and took her lover away.

He went to a school heap big
But her voice called to him from the west
   The gray goose and quail
   O'er the steep, rugged trail
Rekindled love for the wild in his breast.

The books on the table faded away
By the river there stood a tepee
   Then plain to his view
   Sitting in a canoe
Was the maiden he longed so to see.

Now the scene quickly changes; a vast forest stood
Run over with the fox and the bear,
   The hunter brought moose
   To his squaw and papoose,
The voices through the mist reached him there.

In a wigwam that day she prayed in her way
"Great Spirit alone, hear my plea
   While here on my knees
   I beg of you, please
Send back my loved one to me."

A call he could not resist
Grew stronger each day in his breast
   So swiftly down stream
   To the girl of his dreams
He glided out to the golden west.

Away from his new found world
He declared civilization a bother
   Traded his books
   For fish lines and hooks
And returned to the land of his father.

THE CLIFF BY THE SEA

I'd love to stand upon a cliff
And watch the rolling sea,
Follow the gulls on their long flight
Sailing out gracefully.
While the wind in it's wild glee
Caressed my cheeks and hair
I'd love to live close by the sea
And in all it's beauty share.

And as I stood upon this cliff
To watch the ships go by,
Away from all the din and noise
With just the sea birds cry.
The grandeur would enthrall me
As the waves dash from cave to rock
Billowing in their mad rush
Lashing against the dock.

I now picture this wonderful sight
The sky and majestic sea,
Whose depths we do but vaguely know
But wherein lie mysteries.
And now comes a murmur soft and low
On the crest of a foamy wave
It may be the spirit of a soul
Who went down in a watery grave.

I cannot stand on yonder cliff
And be bathed in the sun's bright ray
But I can be in tune with nature's law
That brings happiness day by day.
I'd love to climb to greater heights
Where I could stand alone
A place of understanding
Develops as I roam.

It may not be upon a cliff
Where the ships go sailing by,
But I shall climb to a sphere
That reaches beyond the sky.
And tho' I stumble many times
I'll at last reach the plane
Above the sea and lofty cliff
Where my spirit shall be happy again.

| 53 |

IF I WERE AN ARTIST

If I had the gift of an artist
 I would paint the land and sea,
The mountains and the rocky caves
 With all their charms for thee.
I would travel to the frozen north
 And paint a glacier snowy white,
The stars that give a silvery touch
 And the sun setting out of sight.

I'd climb to the mountain peaks
 To paint this vast land of ours
The purple lining of the clouds
 Rose and silver after the showers.
I would go down through the valley
 Where are nooks, rocks, and rills
I would paint each little crevice
 And for background, the verdant hills.

And then I'd paint the shepherd
 Watching over his sheep
As they graze on the mossy hillside
 And the little lambs fast asleep.
The ocean in all it's grandeur
 And the waves tossed into foam
I would paint all that is beautiful
 And take it with me back home.

I just would never stop painting
 Not even to take a rest;
I would wander thru all the woods
 And paint the bird and her nest.
I would paint the beautiful roses
 With fragrance that fills the air,
The modest shrinking violets
 And the pond lillies so fair.

Indeed all the flowery kingdom
 I'd portray with artful hand,
I'd paint and paint forever
 And fulfill my soul's demand.

THE CRUMBLING WALLS
of
THE OLD CASTLE ON THE HILL

If you will come and go with me,
    I'll take you thru an ancient hall,
I'll show you paintings of art
    Hanging on the embossed wall
Ladies gay, and of other days,
    With frills and bustles high,
Hats with feathers much bedecked,
    Pulled o'er their eyes so shy.

And down the coridor we'll see,
    The bold brave Knights of old,
Who were renowned for valiant deeds,
    As well as lovers bold,
They shed their blood for honor,
    And would quickly flash their swords,
To avenge the slightest insult,
    Without a needless waste of words.

And in this weird Castle,
    You will find cobwebs and mold,
And in the bridal chamber,
    Stands a bed of antique gold;
There sat at this dressing table,
    Many a bride sweet and fair,
Looking at her toilet articles,
    Here's a curl of one's platinum hair.

Dresses worn and much betattered,
    Carpets molded on the floor,
And here is a lady's footstool,
    Just inside the door;
Everything is damp and musty,
    Like the vaults over there,
Where the dead have long been resting,
    Freed from all worldly care.

If you'll press that little button,
    The door will swing silently back,
Look down that dingy stairway,
    You'll find the wine cellar black;
Come, shall we return once more,
    And view the pictures on the wall,
Where the spirit of the dead lingers
    In the crumbling Castle Hall.

ALONG LIFE'S HIGHWAY

I'd like to live beside the road,
  Where folks go passing by,
Would like to have them know,
  That on me they could rely;
I would like to help the needy,
  That pass along my way,
To feel that I could do some good,
  Each and every day.

Should some weary traveler,
  Pass my humble door,
I would make him welcome,
  And give him of my store,
Invite him to enter in,
  And sup with me and mine,
Share our humble board,
  And rest in God's sunshine.

Should a man old and gray,
  With head bowed down so low,
Come trudging along the Highway,
  Steps faltering and slow;
I'd give him food and shelter,
  Help him on his way,
Encourage, not ignore him,
  Make happier his day.

Kind words are so precious,
  A smile goes far, my dear,
It will avert many tragedies,
  And fill the heart with cheer;
There is the motherless child,
  Whose life has just begun,
I'd take her to my cottage,
  And love the little one.

We must be more charitable,
  Glad to share our daily bread,
With those whose sad future,
  Is faced with fear and dread;
Oh show to us our duty, Lord,
  Matter not what may befall,
Create love in our hearts,
  And sympathy for all.

AN ANCIENT LOVE STORY

This story was told in Babylon,
A city of ancient and great renown.
There lived a beautiful maiden fair,
With burnished, golden, curly hair.
 There came a prince of noble birth,
 Whose eyes were kindled with youthful mirth;
 He was presented to her at court,
 And afterward became her escort.

Though surrounded by tutors whose highest aim
Was to teach him history of ancient fame,
Of knights that rode on handsome steeds,
And were highly honored for their brave deeds.
 His heart upon this maid did dwell,
 And his love for her he could not quell.
 So down through the garden of roses they went,
 On innocent youthful pleasure bent.

He kissed her lips, her eyes, her hair,
And told her she was wondrous fair,
Her form swaying with willowy grace,
As they strolled from place to place.
 And thus he wooed the little maid;
 Under a canopy of roses they found shade.
 By their lingering glances one could see,
 Their love would live through eternity.

To tell of the love that was consuming his soul,
He'd carry her away like the knights of old,
To his home under moss-covered bowers,
To live in the midst of beautiful flowers.
 They were enmeshed in the web of love,
 As the stars twinkled o'er them from above.
 He kissed her brow and caressed her hair,
 As though in the wildest of despair.

The darkening shadows soon must fall,
And the maid for her mate will ever call;
The sky will not always be aglow,
Nor the rippling waters gently flow.
 A messenger came—he was called away,
 To fight as his ancestors did. There he lay,
 With upturned face to the beautiful sky
 He was dying, and to the wind whispered "Goodbye".

The wind would waft it back to his love,
And tell her he'd wait for her above,
And if she would be in the rose garden at seven,
He would peep at her through the curtains in Heaven.
 The wind gave a sigh as it blew away;
 A sad message for her it had to convey,
 And found her standing by the rose garden gate,
 Wondering why her lover was late.

(Continued on following page)

AN ANCENT LOVE STORY—(Continued)

Her form shook with sobs as she walked to the bower;
The perfume was exuding from her favorite flower.
On the bench she watched the sky, with tears unshed;
When morning came, her spirit too had fled:
Who knows but he, when at the hour of seven,
while peeping at her through the curtains of Heaven,
Drew her soul upward to him once more,
To be with each other as heretofore?

COME WALK AMONG THE FLOWERS

Come walk with me in my Garden,
Of flowers wonderful and rare,
With hues of the rainbow,
Shaded from the sun's bright glare;
Ramblers delicately tinted,
Twine 'round the window ledge,
The evergreen and foliage,
Are like a picturesque hedge.

I love to walk among them,
And inhale sweet perfume,
Exuding from the flowers,
Radiant in their bloom;
Roses, the Queen of Beauty,
Nodding stately heads,
And modest shrinking violets,
Peeping from their beds.

I would have you stroll with me,
Along the primrose walk,
And listen to the flowers,
As they romantically talk;
When you release your thoughts,
Locked within your heart,
They read your inmost secrets,
And to the winds impart.

The wind conveys them softly,
Every sweet and tender word,
The message that you whispered,
Came as fleet as a bird;
And this is what was told to me,
That I enter into your scheme,
When you seek solitude,
Where you dream and dream.

I'd love to have you sit with me,
Where the birds sweetly sing,
And be under their magic spell,
And listen to the blue-bells ring,
Shall I look for you at twilight,
When the evening shadows fall,
I'll be waiting in the garden,
Yearning to hear your call.

[58]

THE RACE TRACK ROMANCE

Yo' shure does make me mighty ti'd
  Talkin' 'bout dat race track,
Grumblin' 'bout yo' bad luck—
  An' de ve'y next day yo' goes back.
Now yo' thinks yo' luck's done changed,
  'Cause yo' found dat fo' leaf clover;
'Lows yo'se gwine put ebry cent
  On de hoss called Captain Rover.

Yo' is de mos' uncertainest man
  Dat I eber seed in my life.
I feared I'se made a monstrous mistake
  'Ceptin' myself as yo' wife.
Dar's times I looks 'way back,
  When I was sweet and young—
I sho' was good lookin' den;
  In dem days yo' warn't so low flung.

Who's dat crossin' de fork ob de road?
  Ain't dat Sister Malindy Slack?
Ah hears dat she's done cut loose,
  An' is offen seed at dat race track.
Here she comes 'round de house;
  She's closed dat garden gate.
Wondah why she's walkin' so fas';
  Acts like she feared ob ebin' late.

Uh huh! Hit certainly am mighty strange;
  What does she want 'roun' hyar today,
When all de women am a-workin'?
  Huh! She's too ole for a dress dat gay.
Why yo' puttin' on dem dar pants fur,
  An' dem shoes wid dem low spats?
Whar does yo' specs yo's gwine to?
  What for yo' tryin' on so many hats?

Open dat do', George Washington Brown!
  Why, come right in, Miss Malinda Slack!
My, yo' mus' be gwine away;
  It shorely cain't be to de track.
Why, yo' is sort of nervous lak;
  Yo' face is pale as hit can be.
Come ovah by de winder hyar,
  An' have a little talk wid me.

(Dat woman didn't spec' to fin' me hyar.) (Aside)

I's sorry we'se done eat our dinner;
  I 'spec', dough, yo' has had yourn too.
Yo' face ain't lookin' so very cheerful.
  What's de matter, does yo' feel blue?
Yo' said yo' was jus' out walkin',
  An' wanted me foh to see yo' dress.
I think it gran' an' lubly,
  But jist a little tight across de ches'.

(Continued on following page)

THE RACE TRACK ROMANCE—(Continued)

Jist den I heard a rumblin' noise,
    Lak a purson fallin' down;
I looked to see what de trouble wus,
    And dar lay George Washington Brown,
His face dun turned right ashy;
    A letter dun fell out of one of his pockets;
He grabbed at hit, den fell ag'in,
    His eyes mos' poppin' out of de sockets.

(Drat him, says I, drat him.)   (Aside)

Den I stopped an' picked hit up,
    An' read dat letter throo and throo;
Malinda callin' him baby names,
    Telling him she was awfully blue,
An' she would jist haf to seed him,
    (Her baby)   (Aside)
    For jist a little while,
Dat she was comin' over to de house
    To show him some fancy style.

(Huh! See dat?)   (Aside)

Dey knowed right den dat de jig wus up;
    On George's face wus a sickly grin;
Malinda she done wipe her eyes,
    As deceitful as home made sin.
Den I said to bofe ob dem:
    "Yo' shorely is low flung.
Befo' I would a-done sich a thing
    I'd on my sef some trouble brung."

Den I said: "George Washington Brown,
    I's gwine to forgive yo' dis hyer time,
But don' let me catch yo' no mo'
    Vampin' Malindy or Emeline."
Den I turned to speak my min'
    To dat no 'count Malinda Slack,
But she was beatin' de dust for shore—
    All I c'ud see wus her back.

Well, dat cured him ob de races;
    I hears no mo' about de track;
He still looks kind o' sheepish, do.
    (Yo knows what I means)   (Aside)
    Kine a-uneasy lak.
Whenever he looks up in my face
    Dar's sompin' he wants to say;
But he rolls his eyes, and turns away,
    Foh he's thankful to see another day.

THE ENVIOUS NEIGHBOR

Ain't dat old Sister Ruggie?
Looks like her funny face;
It's de same old hoss and buggy,
Keepin' up de same old pace.

I ain't gwine to show my s'prise,
'Case she's got dat Easter bonnet on:
Anybody kin see 'tain't becomin' her eyes;
I wonder if it's so her husband's gone.

I knows when she didn't have de clo'se
Like she now puts on her back:
It's hard to git use to folks like dose.
I wonder why she was out wif ole man Black.

Seems to me she acts mighty pert
In de las' few years.
'Co'se I ain't sayin' dat she flirts,
I'se just tellin' you' how it 'pears.

HARVEST TIME

De fros am on de punkin,
An it am on de vine;
It am time to pick persimmons,
It am also huskin' time;
It am time to pick muscadines,
Dat hangs frum de trees,
It am time to hunt for gubbers,
An gather in de sheaves.

It am time to gather pawpaws,
Time to look fur de coon;
Who lobes to hide amung de leves,
An furgits about de moon—
Dat am shinin' down so brite,
Among de leves in de tree,
Showin up po Mr. Coon,
As plain as plain can be.

An den dars Mr. Possum,
I guess yo herd of him,
His meat am good wid taters,
Yo cotch him when de moon am dim;
Den its time to make bonfires,
Fur de little girls an boys,
Rost taters in de ashes,
Its de fun dey sho enjoys.

Den its time fur de ole folks,
Wid de rumatiz in de heel,
To go to bed an slumber,
Dats de way ole folks feel.
It am time to sit befo de fire,
It am time to pop de corn,
It am time fur us to make lobe,
An be glad dat we wur born.

[61]

"MAMMY KNOWS."

Cum hyar honey to yo mammy,
  Lay yo hed upon my lap,
Mudder knows dis chile am drowsey,
  Cum along and take a nap.

Den into detrunnel bed
  Mammy's gwine to lay dis chile;
Let him res' his little hed,
  So he kin dream and smile.

'Bout de applies in de orchard,
  And yo little dog dats in de yard.
Yo papa's in de garden,
  Workin' monstrous hard.

So yo mammy kin make hoecakes,
  In de good ole summer time,
When de corn an beans am cookin',
  And we gather grapes fur wine.

Aint dat chile de sweetis thing
  Dat you most eber seed?
Dar aint no mo' 'round hyar like him,
  Lak him—well, no, indeed.

———

I AM A MAD MAN

I'm just as mad as I can be,
And don't nobody bother me,
'Cause my feelings have been hurt—
I found my girl to be a flirt.
I went to see her, the other night;
She made me mad enough to fight—
Sitting on a strange man's knee,
Just as happy as she could be,

Singing, "Daddy, hold me tight,
Just this way, dear, every night;
You've beat the others by a mile
And won the love of this here chil'.
When we were down to the dance,
You showed your love in every glance.
When you're away I am so blue,
'Cause I love my Daddy, 'deed I do."

"Sho said that she would change some day,
But I laughed at her, and turned away.
She says my Daddy sings love songs to me,
And he'll love me through eternity.
You always said you'd like to roam,
So away, man, you have lost your home.
I love my daddy more and more.
When you go out, please shut the door."

[62]

ABOUT THE EDITORS

Henry Louis Gates, Jr., is the W. E. B. Du Bois Professor of the Humanities, Chair of the Afro-American Studies Department, and Director of the W. E. B. Du Bois Institute for Afro-American Research at Harvard University. One of the leading scholars of African-American literature and culture, he is the author of *Figures in Black: Words, Signs, and the Racial Self* (1987), *The Signifying Monkey: A Theory of Afro-American Literary Criticism* (1988), *Loose Canons: Notes on the Culture Wars* (1992), and the memoir *Colored People* (1994).

Jennifer Burton is in the Ph.D. program in English Language and Literature at Harvard University. She is the volume editor of *The Prize Plays and Other One-Acts* in this series. She is a contributor to *The Oxford Companion to African-American Literature* and to *Great Lives from History: American Women*. With her mother and sister she coauthored two one-act plays, *Rita's Haircut* and *Litany of the Clothes*. Her fiction and personal essays have appeared in *Sun Dog, There and Back*, and *Buffalo*, the Sunday magazine of the *Buffalo News*.

Mary Anne Stewart Boelcskevy is in the Ph.D. program in English Language and Literature at Harvard University. She has served on the editorial research staff for the *Norton Anthology of African-American Literature* (1996), and her work has appeared in *The Cambridge History of American Literature, Volume Eight: Poetry and Criticism since 1940* (1996).